The King's Arcadia:
Inigo Jones and the Stuart Court

A quatercentenary exhibition held at the Banqueting House, Whitehall
from July 12th to September 2nd, 1973

Catalogue by
John Harris, Stephen Orgel and Roy Strong

Arts Council of Great Britain   1973

Exhibition designed by Michael Brawne
Installation by Beck and Pollitzer Limited
Photographic blow-ups by Brook-Tella Limited
Models by Bruce Rowling of Thurloe Models Limited
and Philip Wood
Catalogue edited by Janet Holt

Catalogue designed by Graham Johnson/Lund Humphries
and printed by Lund Humphries, London and Bradford

Contents

Part III The King's Arcadia

Preface

The Arts Council has organised this exhibition to celebrate the 400th anniversary of the birth of Inigo Jones. It also coincides with the magnificent restoration of the Banqueting House in Whitehall, designed by him, now in the care of the Department of the Environment and the publication of the new complete catalogue *raisonné* of his drawings for the stage, *Inigo Jones, The Theatre of the Stuart Court* by Stephen Orgel and Roy Strong.

The Banqueting House is not only a suitable location for this exhibition as the heart of the Stuart Court for which Jones created the majority of his works, but is also the key exhibit, and we appreciate the co-operation of the Department of the Environment in allowing us to hold the exhibition. We have received the most generous support from all owners, but special mention must be made of the three main collections of Inigo Jones drawings, the Duke of Devonshire's collection at Chatsworth, the Provost and Fellows of Worcester College, Oxford and the President and Council of the Royal Institute of British Architects. Without the full co-operation of the Duke of Devonshire and his Librarian, Mr Thomas Wragg, of Dr Richard Sayce, Librarian of Worcester College, and of Mr John Harris of the Royal Institute of British Architects, this exhibition would not have been possible. Once again, Her Majesty The Queen has graciously allowed us to borrow paintings from the Royal Collection. A list of all lenders is on page 224 of this catalogue.

We thank Dr Roy Strong, Mr John Harris and Professor Stephen Orgel, from whom the idea for this exhibition emanated. They have been responsible for the selection of the material and the preparation of the catalogue. The organisers greatly appreciate the contributions made to the catalogue by Mr H. M. Colvin, Mr Malcolm Pinhorn and Dr Gordon Toplis. Among the many others who have been very helpful, especial thanks are due to: Mr Alan Argent, Mr Lionel Bell, Mr Geoffrey de Bellaigue, Mrs Anne Cushion, Mrs Nina Drummond, Mr R. G. Emberson, Miss Wendy Hefford, Mr Klaus Henning, Mrs Jill Lever, Miss Pamela Lewis, Miss Jane Macausland, Mr Oliver Millar, Miss Lesley Montgomery, Mr Howard Nixon, Mr George Pearce, Mrs Margaret Richardson, Mrs Margaret Richards, Miss M. Sherman, Miss Jennifer Sherwood, Mr P. A. Stocker, Sir John Summerson, Mr Alan Tait, Miss Anne Turner, Mr R. Williams.

Robin Campbell
Director of Art

Norbert Lynton
Director of Exhibitions

Foreword

This exhibition sets out to re-discover and to re-define Inigo Jones within his own age. As a Renaissance *uomo universale*, the ideal Vitruvian architect-engineer, his activities span practically every field of the arts in early seventeenth-century England. Jones was an architect, painter, engineer, designer, connoisseur, collector, author, theoretician and, at the same time, a remarkably coherent intellect. Mostly he is viewed as a fragmented personality, depending upon whether one's main interest is in his architectural or theatrical achievements. This exhibition deliberately, through the happy collaboration of experts in both fields, attempts to re-establish him as a single figure. For Jones a court masque was as important and as significant as a building, for both were direct expressions of the harmonic principles which governed his creations. This has been the guiding thesis which has enabled us to re-create in his quatercentenary year *The King's Arcadia*.

John Harris, Stephen Orgel, Roy Strong

Chronology: Inigo Jones

1573 Birth of Inigo Jones

1598–1601 Possibly travelled in the train of Lord Roos (later sixth Earl of Rutland) to France, Germany and Italy

1603 To Denmark with 5th Earl of Rutland

1604 Return to England, in service of Queen Anne

1605 *The Masque of Blackness* January 6th
Plays at Oxford: *Alba, Ajax Flagellifer* August 28th, *Vertumnus* August 29th, *Arcadia Reformed* (*The Queen's Arcadia*) August 30th

1606 *Hymenaei* January 6th

1607 *The Lord Hay's Masque* January 6th; Entertainment for James I at Theobalds: *The Penates*

1608 Design for the New Exchange or 'Britain's Burse'; Restoration of central tower of St. Paul's Cathedral; *The Haddington Masque* 6th–11th May; Entertainment given by Lord Salisbury

1609 *The Masque of Queens* February 2nd; Entertainment given by Lord Salisbury at the opening of Britain's Burse; Visits France

Chronology: other events

1573 Peace of Constantinople between Turkey and Venice; Ben Jonson b.

1574 Charles IX of France d., succeeded by Henry III

1576 Frobisher annexes Frobisher Bay; Titian d.

1577 Francis Drake circumnavigates the world; Rubens b.

1578 James VI of Scotland takes over government

1580 Andrea Palladio d.

1581 James VI signs second Scottish Confession of Faith; English Act imposing heavy fines for Catholic recusancy

1584 William of Orange assassinated; Maurice of Nassau succeeds as Stadtholder

1588 Defeat of the Spanish Armada

1589 Henry III of France d. succeeded by Henry IV

1592 Jacques Callot b.

1596 Pietro da Cortona b.

1598 Philip II of Spain d., succeeded by Philip III; Gianlorenzo Bernini b.

1599 James VI: *Basilikon Doron*, condemns Presbyterianism and asserts Divine Right of Kings; Francesco Borromini b.; Anthony Van Dyck b.; Shakespeare *Julius Caesar*; Juan de Mariana *De Rege et Regis Institutione* justifies tyrannicide

1600 Shakespeare *Henry V, As You Like It, Much Ado*; Jonson *Every Man out of His Humour*; James VI appoints three titular bishops in Scotland; East India Company established

1601 First voyage of East India Company ships; Shakespeare *Twelfth Night, Troilus and Cressida*; Jonson *Every Man in His Humour*

1602 Shakespeare *Merry Wives of Windsor*; Bodleian Library opened

1602–4 Galileo discovers laws of gravitation and oscillation

1603 Elizabeth d., James VI proclaimed King James I of England, France and Ireland; James I grants toleration to Roman Catholics; Henry IV calls Jesuits back to France; Shakespeare *All's Well That Ends Well, Hamlet*; Accademia dei Lincei, Rome, founded; Joh. Althusius *Politics Methodice Digesta* theory of Monarchomachism

1604 Peace between England and Spain; Spaniards capture Ostend; Shakespeare *Othello, Measure for Measure*; Rob. Cawdrey *Table Alphabetical*, first English dictionary

1605 Gunpowder Plot discovered; Place des Vosges (Royale) begun; Shakespeare *King Lear, Macbeth*; Bacon *Advancement of Learning*; Cervantes *Don Quixote* pt.i. (Engl. transl. 1612)

1606 First Charter of Virginia for London and Plymouth companies; Galileo invents proportional compass; Shakespeare *Anthony and Cleopatra*

1607 Place Dauphine (Henry IV) begun; Shakespeare *Timon of Athens*; Jonson *Volpone*; Monteverdi *Orfeo* (opera); English settlements in Virginia; Jamestown founded

1608 Treaty for mutual defence between England and Netherlands; Shakespeare *Coriolanus*

1609 Twelve years' truce between Spain and Netherlands; Netherlands ally with England and France for 12 years

1610 Prince Henry's *Barriers* January 6th; *Accession Day Tilt: Elephant Pageant* March 24th; *Tethys' Festival* June 5th; *Creation Tilt* for Prince Henry

1611 Becomes Surveyor to Henry, Prince of Wales; *Oberon, The Fairy Prince* January 1st; *Love Freed from Ignorance and Folly* February 3rd

1613 *The Lords' Masque* February 14th; *The Memorable Masque of the Middle Temple and Lincoln's Inn* February 15th; Travels to Italy in the train of Thomas, Earl of Arundel

1615 Returns and succeeds as Surveyor of Works; *The Golden Age Restored*

1615–17 Newmarket brewhouse, stable, dog house and riding house stables for Sir Thomas Compton and Mr Duppa; the period of transitional works

1616 Begins work on the Queen's House, Greenwich, for Anne of Denmark; *Mercury Vindicated*

1617 *The Vision of Delight* January 6th, repeated January 19th

1617–18 St. James's Palace, the Princes's Buttery; Somerset House, lantern over the hall; Oatlands Palace, the park and vineyard gateways, probably three other gateways, and the silkworm room; Star Chamber designs

1618 *Pleasure Reconciled to Virtue* January 6th; *For the Honour of Wales* February 17th

1619 Lost Masque for Prince Charles, January 6th; Hearse for Queen Anne's funeral

1619–20 The Marquess of Buckingham's Second Lodging at Whitehall

1619–22 The Banqueting House, Whitehall

1619–21 The Prince's Lodging and Clerk of Works' House at Newmarket

---

1620 *News from the New World* January 7th repeated February 29th; *Pan's Anniversary* June 19th; investigated Stonehenge

1620–21 Additions to the Countess of Buckingham's Lodging, Whitehall

1621 Lost Masque for Prince Charles, January 6th

1622 *The Masque of Augurs* January 6th repeated May 6th

1623 *Time Vindicated to Himself and to His Honours* January 19th

1623–25 The Queen's Chapel at St. James's remodelling of the Elizabethan chapel and Great Gate in the park at Greenwich Palace

1623–24 Stables at Theobalds Palace; New ceiling for the House of Lords

1624 Park Stairs at Whitehall Palace; *Neptune's Triumph for the Return of Albion* planned for January 6th, cancelled due to dispute over ambassadorial precedence; Prince Charles returns from Spain

1625 *The Fortunate Isles and their Union* January 9th; Banqueting House at Theobalds Palace; alterations to Dover Castle; catafalque for James I's funeral

1626 A clock house at Whitehall; Queen's Cabinet Room at Somerset House; *Artenice* February 21st

1627 Park Gate at St. James's; Lost masque for the Queen

1628 Lost masque for the King intended for Shrovetide 1628; John Webb becomes pupil

1628–31 River Stairs at Somerset House

1629 The Whitehall Cockpit

1629–31 Queen's Withdrawing Chamber, pergula window and a sculpture gallery in the garden of St. James's

---

1630–38 Completion and decoration of Queen's House at Greenwich

1630–35 The Chapel at Somerset House

1631 A garden arbour at Oatlands Palace, park gate at St. James's; *Love's Triumph through Callipolis* January 9th; *Chloridia* February 22nd; Covent Garden Development; Hale Church

1631–32 Lodge in Bagshot Park

1610 Henry IV allies with German Protestant Union; Henry IV assassinated; succeeded by Louis XIII (–1643) under regency of Marie de Medici, his mother, until 1617; Shakespeare *Cymbeline*; William Dobson b.

1611 Shakespeare *Winter's Tale*; John Webb b.; Authorised version of Bible issued

1612 Robert Cecil d.; Henry, Prince of Wales d.; Scots Parliament confirms restoration of Episcopacy; two Unitarians burnt in England; last time heretics were burnt; Shakespeare *Tempest*; Rubens *Decent from the Cross*

1613 Elizabeth, daughter of James I, marries Frederick V, Elector Palatine; Shakespeare *Henry VIII*; Cervantes *Novelas Ejemplares*; Domenico Theotocopoulos (El Greco) d.

1613–18 Bodleian Library, Oxford, built by Thos. Holt

1614 Napier invents logarithms

1616 Shakespeare d. at Stratford; Cevantes d. in Madrid. Bernini *Apollo and Daphne* his first work; Vicenzo Scamozzi d.

1617 Isaac Oliver d.

1618 Outbreak of the Thirty Years' War; negotiations for the marriage of Charles to the Infanta of Spain; Raleigh beheaded; English West Africa Company founded, occupies Gambia and Gold Coast

1619 Death of Anne of Denmark; Dulwich College founded by Edward Alleyn; Nicholas Hilliard d.

1620 Pilgrim Fathers leave Plymouth in the Mayflower; New Plymouth founded

1620–21 Van Dyck pays his first visit to England

1621 Philip III of Spain d. succeeded by Philip IV

1622 First English ambassador to Turkey

1622–5 Ruben's *Medici cycle* for the Luxembourg Palace; Paul van Somer d.

1623 Charles Prince of Wales at Madrid; fails to secure betrothal to Spanish princess; publication of the Shakespeare First Folio; Raphael cartoons purchased by Prince Charles

1624 England declares war on France; Richelieu becomes First Minister (–1642) marriage treaty between Charles and Henrietta Maria, sister of Louis XIII of France

1625 James I and VI d.; succeeded by Charles I (–1649): Charles I marries Henrietta Maria of France; Maurice of Nassau d. succeeded by Frederick Henry as Stadtholder; defeat of Huguenots under Soubise who flees to England; Parliament grants tonnage and poundage to Charles I for one year; Act of Revocation, to recover church property in Scotland for national use

1626 Peace of La Rochelle ends Huguenot revolt; Second Parliament; Charles continues to levy tonnage and poundage, and collects Forced Loan

1627 Huguenots revolt again; Richelieu begins siege of La Rochelle, which the English fail to relieve; Duke of Mantua d., his collection purchased by Charles I

1628 Petition of Right, against arbitrary imprisonment, martial law, forced loans, billeting of soldiers and sailors; Duke of Buckingham assassinated; La Rochelle capitulates; Wm. Harvey *De Motu Cordis et Sanguinis*, discovers double circulation of blood

1629 Peace of Susa between England and France; Rubens visits England; Corneille *Melite*; Carlo Maderna d., Bernini appointed architect of St. Peter's Rome

1629–40 The so-called Eleven Years' Tyranny: Charles I rules without Parliament

---

1630 Treaty of Madrid ends war between England and Spain

1632 The cistern at Somerset House; *Albion's Triumph* January 8th; *Tempe Restored* February 14th

1633 Work commenced on St. Paul's cathedral; *The Shepherd's Paradise* January 9th, repeated probably February 2nd, Lower Court Somerset House

1634 *The Faithful Shepherdess; The Triumph of Peace* February 3rd; *Coelum Britannicum* February 18th; *Love's Mistress* November; a Lodge in Hyde Park

1635 *The Temple of Love* February 10th; *Florimène* December 21st; a balcony at Oatlands Palace

1635–36 Remodelling of the Cross Gallery at Somerset House

1636 Design for a chimney piece at Oatlands Palace; Winchester Cathedral Screen; Temple Bar Designs; plays at Oxford *The Floating Island*; *The Royal Slave* August 29th and September 3rd

1637 A new masquing room at Whitehall; a ceiling at Oatlands Palace; the new Cabinet Room at Somerset House.

1638 *Britannia Triumphans* January 17th; *Luminalia* February 6th; *Aglaura*; *The Passionate Lovers*

1639 Alterations to Wimbledon House

1640 *Salmacida Spolia.* January 21st, February 16th, 17th or 18th; *The Queen of Aragon* April 9th & 10th

1645 Taken prisoner at the siege of Basing House

1652 Dies at Somerset House; buried in St. Benet's Church

1632 Van Dyck settles in England; Galileo Galilei *Dialogo sopra; due massimi sistemi del mondo*; Rembrandt *The Lesson in Anatomy*; Van Dyck settles in England as Court Painter

1633 Charles I crowned King of Scotland at Edinburgh; Laud becomes Archbishop of Canterbury; first English factory in Bengal

1634 First writ of ship-money in London to make the King independent of Parliament

1635 Second writ of ship-money, extended to the whole kingdom; enlargement of Royal forests; Jacques Callot d.; Ruben's ceiling installed in the Banqueting House

1636 Pope sends agent to Queen of England; Scottish Council orders use of new Service Book

1637 Charles attempts to introduce new prayer Book into Scotland; outbreak of religious rebellion in Scotland; Ben Jonson d.

1637–38 Ship-money case of John Hampden

1639 General Assembly abolishes Episcopacy in Scotland

1640 Short Parliament – Apr 13–May 5; Nov 3 Long Parliament meets; Dec 11, Root and Branch Petition; Rubens d.

1641 Lord Strafford beheaded; Star Chamber and High Commission Court abolished; Grand Remonstrance; Descartes *Meditationes de Prima Philosophis*; Lely comes to England; Van Dyck d.

1642 Charles attempts to arrest Five Members; Royal standard raised at Nottingham; beginning of English Civil War; Richelieu d.; Cardinal Mazarin becomes First Minister (–1661); John de Critz d.; Hobbes *De Cive*; Theatres closed in England till 1660; Rembrandt *Night Watch*; Galileo d.; Guido Reni d.

1643 Louis XIII d., succeeded by Louis XIV (–1715)

1644 Royalists defeated at Marston Moor; Milton *Areopagitca*; Descartes *Principia Philosophiae*

1645 Cromwell defeats Royalists at Naseby; Archbishop Laud beheaded; Sir Thomas Fairfax appointed commander of Parliamentary army

1646 Charles surrenders to Scottish army at Newark; William Dobson d.

1647 Scots sell Charles to Parliament for £400,000; Frederick Henry, Dutch Stadtholder d.; succeeded by William II; Parliamentary army defeats Irish at Dangan Hill

1648 Pride's Purge of House of Commons; Scots begin Second Civil War; Cromwell defeats Scots at Preston; Outbreak of the Fronde in France (–1653)

1649 Charles I beheaded; Cromwell suppresses revolt of Levellers; Cromwell sacks Drogheda and Wexford, Ireland; England declared Free Commonwealth

---

1650 Cromwell defeats Scots at Dunbar; William II of Netherlands d.; Edinburgh Castle surrenders to Cromwell

1651 Charles II crowned at Scone; Cromwell defeats Charles at Worcester; Charles escapes to France; Hobbes: *Leviathan, or, the Matter, Form and Authority of Government*

1652 Act of Pardon and Oblivion, to reconcile Royalists

Catalogue Note

All drawings exhibited are by Inigo Jones unless otherwise stated. Full description of media is given. Measurements are in centimetres; the height precedes the width. A full bibliography is given at the end of the catalogue and the bibliographical references in the catalogue entries are given to ensure the easy identification of works at a later date. The following abbreviations have been used in this catalogue. Each entry is initialled by its author:

J.H.	John Harris
S.O.	Stephen Orgel
R.S.	Roy Strong
O&S	Stephen Orgel and Roy Strong, *Inigo Jones – The Theatre of the Stuart Court*, 1973
S&B	P. Simpson and C. F. Bell, 'Designs by Inigo Jones for Masques and Plays at Court', *Walpole Society*, XII, 1923–4
Whinney	Margaret Whinney, 'John Webb's drawings for Whitehall Palace', *Walpole Society*, XXXI, 1946
B.M.	The British Museum
P.R.O.	Public Record Office
R.I.B.A.	Royal Institute of British Architects

Part 1: Jones in the Making

The Early Years: 1573–1605

Inigo Jones's Family

Very little is known about the early life of Inigo Jones. We have a few facts and a myriad of legends. The earliest fact is the record of his baptism in the church of St. Bartholomew's the Less, Smithfield, on July 19th, 1573 (1). He was probably one of eight children, several of whom, including a brother, Philip, did not survive infancy. Inigo was named after his father, who possibly married in 1569. Unfortunately, no marriages were recorded in the registers for that year, but in August 1570 a daughter, Millicent, was christened, and buried in May the year after. Inigo was presumably the eldest surviving child and the registers record other events in the life of the Jones family. Philip was born in 1575 and lived for a month. An unnamed daughter was born in February 1576 and was buried in July 1577. Inigo's grandmother, Anne Jones, was buried on March 26th, 1576 and in September 1578 another child, Anne, was christened.

The architect's father, who was also named Inigo, is said to have come from Denbighshire in North Wales, although his grandmother, Anne Jones, was buried at St. Bartholomew's in 1576. An unidentified Jones family 'of Grothkenan', Denbighshire, who used armorial bearings similar to those found on a portrait of the architect, claimed to be related; these arms are almost identical to those of the Trevor family, for whom Inigo Jones is said to have built Plas Teg in Flintshire.

The surname of the architect's father was usually spelt Jones in the parish records, but occasionally Jhones, Johnes or Joanes. There has been some speculation as to the possible origin of the unusual forename Inigo. According to the parish register the architect was, in fact, christened Enego, but, in contemporary records, it is also found as Enigo, Ennigo, Enygo, Ennico, and even Indigo, while Ignatius is found as the latin form. A kinsman was christened Luigo.

From the Poor Rate, the architect's father left the parish of St. Bartholomew in about 1585 and it was probably at this time that he moved to the parish of St. Benet, where he made his will in February 1596. Inigo Jones the Elder was a clothworker and his will reveals few details other than he was to be buried in the chancel of St. Benet's next to his wife. The Jones family thereafter remain an enigma. There is a fleeting reference in 1613 to a payment 'to Mrs. Johnes, for her brother, Mr. Inego Johnes' in the accounts of the Middle Temple and Lincoln's Inn Masque, performed on February 15th, 1613.

The architect did not marry; in his will, made in July 1650, while he was living in the parish of St. Martin in the Fields, Middlesex, he requests to be buried at St. Benet's. He died on June 21st, 1652, at Somerset House and was buried on June 26th in accordance with his wishes. He left one hundred pounds for his funeral expenses and another hundred pounds 'for the erecting of a Monument in memorie of me, to be made of White Marbell, and sett upp in the Church (of St Benet)'. The monument was duly erected against the north wall of the nave but was damaged during the Great Fire of London in 1666 and destroyed when the church was rebuilt by Sir Christopher Wren between 1677 and 1683. Jones also left £500 to Richard Gammon, who married Elizabeth Jones, possibly a cousin; £100 to Mary Wagstaff, described as a kinswoman and £2,000 to Anne, his kinswoman who married John Webb, Jones's assistant. (R.S.)

Early Travels of Inigo Jones 1598?–1604?

Jones's lost years are reminiscent of Shakespeare's and any explanation is largely conjecture based on fragments found in his posthumously published book on Stonehenge (141, 142). In 1605 he was referred to as 'a great Traveller' and in 1613 Jones accompanied the Earl and Countess of Arundel to Italy 'by means of his language and experience in those parts'. Italy in the nineties attracted noblemen of the generation of Queen Elizabeth I's favourite, the Earl of Essex, and it is probably that Jones would have travelled in a nobleman's train. A talented young man who wished to study, as he said in *Stonehenge Restored*, 'the Arts of Design' would have had a natural desire to visit Italy. Later, the same source states, he was called out of Italy to enter into the service of Anne of Denmark's brother, Christian IV. This is possibly an over-simplification of his wanderings which may, it is suggested, be more satisfactorily explained by his links with the Earl of Rutland's family. If the accounts of the early patronage of the Manners family can be accepted, Jones's early years may be conjectured thus:

1597 In London on the death of his father. Possibly he was already an apprentice in the studio of one of the portrait painters of the day such as Marcus Gheeraerts.

1598 Attracted to the service of a young nobleman, probably Francis Manners, Lord Roos, brother of Roger, 5th Earl of Rutland. Lord Roos left England that year for a tour through France, Germany and Italy and was entertained both by the Emperor Mathias and the Archduke Ferdinand. Jones was long enough in Italy to learn to speak Italian fluently. At this period his primary study would have been painting and not architecture.

1603 Back in England, where, in the Earl of Rutland's accounts, it is noted on June 28th, Jones received a payment as a picture-maker for his 'paynes'. Possibly in June and August he travelled in the Earl of Rutland's train to Denmark, to deliver the Order of the Garter to Christian IV. Jones was attracted to the King's service.

1604 By the autumn of 1604, Jones was working with Ben Jonson on the settings and costumes for *The Masque of Blackness* for Anne of Denmark. He had probably returned to England in that year with a letter of introduction to the Queen from her brother. (R.S.)

1 THE BAPTISM OF INIGO JONES, JULY 19TH 1573
Parish Register of St Bartholomew the Less, London
Photograph

Pieter Van Den Keere (*c*.1571–*c*.1624)
2 BIRD'S EYE PLAN OF LONDON, 1593
Engraving in Norden, *Speculum Britanniae*, Part I, 1593
Photograph

The two arrows indicate the two churches associated with the Jones family, St Bartholomew's the Less, Smithfield Wharf, where he was christened, and St Benet, Paul's Wharf, where both he and his father were buried. (R.S.)

3 THE WILL OF INIGO JONES THE ELDER, 14 FEBRUARY 1597
P.R.O., Probate 89/C/4354
Photograph

4 HOUSEHOLD ACCOUNTS FOR 1603 OF ROGER, 5TH EARL OF RUTLAND
Photograph

The arrow indicates the payment to Inigo Jones. (R.S.)

Anonymous

5 FRANCIS MANNERS, LORD ROOS, LATER 6TH EARL OF RUTLAND (1578–1632)
Engraving
Photograph

Anonymous

6 CHRISTIAN IV OF DENMARK
Photograph

The Festival Tradition

When Ben Jonson and Inigo Jones created the first masque for the Stuart Court in 1605, *The Masque of Blackness*, they were using elements from an existing tradition of courtly revelry inherited from the Elizabethans. Elizabeth I was never a lavish patron of the arts and the visual roots of Jones's early productions lie in the chivalrous spectacles staged by the Queen's knights on her Accession Day each year and in the fêtes presented by nobility and gentry in her honour while the Court was on its summer progress. Contemporary visual records of what these spectacles looked like are virtually non-existent and the only glimpses we catch are occasional ones in fancy dress portraits. These confirm that Inigo Jones was working within an existing visual repertory in respect of costumes and could work within an old-fashioned format for scenery. Several of the early designs (32, 66) are for three-dimensional locations, placed in an arena setting within the Elizabethan 'theatre-in-the-round' tradition. They are not designs governed by the proscenium arch and scientific perspective, which was his major visual innovation in 1605. (R.S.)

Anonymous

7 THE MEMORIAL PORTRAIT OF SIR HENRY UNTON, C.1596
Photograph

This picture was painted in memory of Sir Henry Unton (1557?–96), courtier and ambassador, probably at the behest of his widow sometime shortly after his death. It is unique in containing the only known record of an Elizabethan masque being performed. Unton and his wife are shown feasting while the masquers enter in procession, circling around a broken consort who provide the music. The masquers are headed by Mercury and Diana with her hair unbound as a virgin and holding a huntress's bow and arrow. Behind follow her train similarly attired and the torch-bearers are boys in skin-coats of black and white. A presenter gives Lady Unton a paper, on which there would have been verses or a speech explaining the theme of the masque. Court productions would have been more elaborate with pageant cars and three-dimensional settings, but not so different in effect. They were usually prefaced by dialogue and song leading up to the *raison d'être* of the masquers' arrival. After their

7

procession and homage would follow choreographed and then general dancing. The dresses for Diana and her nymphs are consistent in style with those for *Blackness* (39, 40). (R.S.)

Arend van Buchel after Johannes de Witt

8 THE SWAN THEATRE
Photograph

Johannes de Witt, a Dutch traveller, visited London in 1596 or thereabouts, and was particularly impressed with the theatres, which must have been familiar to Jones. He described them in a letter to his friend Arend van Buchel of Utrecht; the Swan especially interested de Witt, because it seemed to him to be based on a Roman model, and he included a drawing of it. The letter and drawing have disappeared, but van Buchel copied them into his commonplace book, and this has survived. There is no way of knowing whether or how van Buchel altered de Witt's original, and there are certain puzzling details in the drawing; but it remains a prime piece of evidence about the Elizabethan theatre. This is the only contemporary representation of the interior of an Elizabethan public playhouse, of which there were only three before the Restoration. It shows a simple platform stage with no scenery and minimal properties, a back façade with two entrances, a gallery above, two elegant columns supporting

9

a roof over the gallery. A scene is in progress, but the only spectators visible are in the gallery. This is one of the puzzling details as the gallery was a playing area, and there is no other evidence that seats were sold there. It has been suggested that what de Witt saw was not a performance but a rehearsal; it is more likely, however, that the figures in the gallery are part of the scene taking place on stage, or alternatively, that they were added by van Buchel, who may not have understood the function of the gallery. The fact that the flag is flying suggests that a performance, not a rehearsal, is in progress. De Witt's letter adds the information that the Swan was the largest and most splendid of the London public theatres; built of flint, with columns painted to look like marble, it has a capacity of three thousand. (s.o.)

Nicholas Hilliard (1547–1619)
9 GEORGE CLIFFORD, 3RD EARL OF CUMBERLAND, C.1590
Miniature
Photograph

George Clifford 3rd Earl of Cumberland (1558–1605) succeeded Sir Henry Lee as Queen's Champion at the tilt in 1590. On that occasion a Temple of the Vestal Virgins had been erected in the tiltyard of Whitehall Palace in honour of Elizabeth I. Cumberland attended the tilts in his guise of the Knight of Pendragon Castle, but the dominant figure in tilt mythology was the Queen's last favourite, Essex. The Accession Day Tilts were the focal point of late Elizabethan festival traditions, a form which found expression in the elaborate entries of knights in fancy dress, come to pay homage

10

to the Queen, to whom each knight presented an emblematic shield. Such a shield can be seen hanging on the tree behind Cumberland to the right. *Impresa* shields were presented in the masques and Inigo Jones invested the masquers in *The Masque of Blackness* with such shields, replaced in the final design by fans. Cumberland's costume is a rare example of Elizabethan fancy dress: star-studded armour, with a surcoat embroidered with an emblematic design consisting of celestial spheres, *caducei* and branches of olive. Inigo Jones must have been familiar with these traditions of courtly chivalry and his own early designs include allegorical costumes for the tournament (68). The public paid to see these spectacles. (R.S.)

Marcus Gheeraerts the Younger (fl. *c*.1615)
10 LADY IN FANCY DRESS
Oil on panel: 216·5 × 135·3
Her Majesty The Queen

This strange allegorical portrait is a rare instance of late Elizabethan fancy dress. It does not specifically relate to a masquerade, but is a complex of allusions to a lady unhappy in her *amours*. Her costume is based on that of a *Persian Virgin* in Boissard's *Habitus Variarum Orbis Gentium*, 1581, with a long loose robe covered with embroidery and a mitre head-dress from which floats a veil. The elongation and stance of the

11

figure does not differ greatly from Jones's earliest designs (39, 46, 49) and suggests the traditional context of the architect's work for court festivals. (R.S.)

Anonymous

11 THE ELVETHAM ENTERTAINMENT, 1591
Wood engraving
Photograph

Apart from the tilts late Elizabethan festivals found their flowering in the entertainments staged for the Queen during her summer progress. These were essentially *pièces d'occasion*, for the most part *al fresco*, designed to complement the Queen and often took the form of a debate leading up to a resolution of opposing parties caused by the Queen's presence. The mythology of these entertainments, like the masques, was a mixture of classical and romantic. Lord Hertford's entertainment at Elvetham in 1591 provides a spectacular instance of these outdoor productions. Elizabeth was welcomed by the Graces and Hours who sprinkled flowers in her path singing of the second spring she had brought; she was awakened one morning by the Fairy Queen and her train dancing beneath her windows, and feasted during a stupendous firework display. But the most splendid of all was the water festival for which there is an illustration. A vast crescent-moon shaped lake had been dug in honour of Elizabeth as the moon goddess ruler of the seas. This was the setting for a dramatic presentation in which Elizabeth rescued a maiden in distress and vanquished a fiery snail-monster which symbolised her political adversaries. This achieved, the gentle deities of sea and land were reconciled by the peace-loving Queen. Inigo Jones worked in his early years within this tradition, staging *fêtes* to honour James I's visits to Robert Cecil, Earl of Salisbury (32). (R.S.)

12

12 JAMES I'S CORONATION ENTRY, 1604
Engraving from Stephen Harrison, *Arches of Triumph*, London, 1604
Photograph

James I's entry into London in March 1604 was the first major entry since 1559. Delayed a year, on account of the plague, it was of unprecedented splendour and the arches designed by Stephen Harrison were manifestations, under the direction of Ben Jonson and Thomas Dekker, of Renaissance classical scholarship. They represent the earliest acknowledged application of the principles of harmonic proportion to architecture in England. Each arch was a series of ratios, the result of reflections which depended directly or indirectly on the Pythagorean-Platonic division of the musical scale. The first arch was of the Tuscan order, 'being the principal pillar of those five upon which the *Noble Frame* of *Architecture* doth stand'. Ben Jonson paraphrases Alberti, who is in turn paraphrasing Vitruvius, in defining these concepts:

'The nature and properties of these Devices being to present alwaies some one entire bodie, or figure, consisting of distinct members, and each of those expressing it selfe, in their owne active sphaere, yet all, with that generall harmonie so connexed, and disposed, as no one little part can be missing to the illustration of the whole . . .'

In this Jonson ironically sums up one of the key principles upon which Inigo Jones based his philosophy as the Vitruvian architect-engineer. It is revealing, that a cursory examination of these engravings with their Netherlandish flourishes and excrescences, would hardly suggest that they were erected according to renaissance humanist architectural theory. They seem to have been directly inspired by those for the entry of the Archduke Albert and the Infanta Isabella into Antwerp in 1599. (R.S.)

17

The Architectural Tradition

When George Chapman dedicated his translation of *Musaeus* to Jones in 1616 he called him 'our only learned architect'. This was probably not fulsome praise. As the new Surveyor of the King's Works, Jones introduced to England the Renaissance concept of the architect as autocrat. Whoever were the 'architects' or 'surveyors' of late Elizabethan prodigy houses, they were rarely able to retain design control of the building from beginning to end. A building grew empirically. Burghley House may have had three architects in the course of its construction, and their ideas were all controlled from the fount of learning, their patron William Cecil. When Sir Thomas Smith visited Paris in 1568, Cecil enquired after a French book on architecture he had seen at Smith's house at Hill Hall. This was probably Du Cerceau's *Plus Excellents Bâtiments de France* of 1576, of which the copy, signed by Cecil, is in Mr. and Mrs. Paul Mellon's collection. Elizabethan architecture grew out of national precepts aided by the standard architectural authors available in the libraries of these Elizabethan men of learning. The 9th Earl of Northumberland wrote to Cecil in 1603 that he was planning to 'see Copthall, for now that I am a builder I must borrow of my knowledge somewhat out of Tibballs [*sic* Theobalds], somewhat out of every place of mark where curiosities are used', and in 1610 he offered to lend Sir John Holles, who already owned Palladio's *I Quattro Libri dell' Architettura*, no less than books by Alberti, Serlio, de L'Orme, Vignola, du Cerçeau and Dietterlin. Architects and surveyors, even one of Smythson's great reputation, must have listened intently to what their patrons had to say, and would have eagerly examined architectural books and prints in the libraries. In addition to these more 'classical' authors, there might have been something by Vredeman de Vries, possibly the *Variae Architecturae Formae* of 1563; certainly an edition of Hans Blum on the orders, which saw many editions and was first translated into English in 1608; and the first English architectural book, John Shute's *The First And Chief Groundes of Architecture* of 1563. Not all Elizabethan patrons owned architectural books, but there is plenty of evidence for an established tradition of borrowing from those who did. The single mind then, behind a single building, was a rarity. The advent of Jones was to transform this practice. (J.H.)

The Architectural Inheritance

13 ENGRAVED VIEW OF OLD SOMERSET HOUSE, STRAND, LONDON
Photograph

Started by the Protector Somerset in 1547, this was the first rationally considered classical façade in England. (J.H.)

14 LONGLEAT, WILTSHIRE
Photograph

Here, Sir John Thynne, once Somerset's steward and confidant, called in Robert Smythson in 1568 to build what is known as 'the third Longleat', but in 1572 it was reconstructed a fourth time using an exterior modulation of pilastered bay windows – for which Smythson's design survives. At Longleat, high Elizabethan classicism was born. (J.H.)

25

15 BURGHLEY HOUSE, NORTHAMPTONSHIRE
Photograph

The north façade, dated 1587, marked the final phase in the rebuilding of the external shell of William Cecil's fantastical monument to Elizabethan self-confidence. (J.H.)

16 WOLLATON HALL, NOTTINGHAMSHIRE
Photograph

Begun in 1580 for Sir Francis Willoughby, this is the house with which Robert Smythson was more personally connected than any other. He lies buried in the nearby churchyard, there described as 'Architector and Survayor unto yee most worthy house of Wollaton'. (J.H.)

17 HARDWICK HALL, DERBYSHIRE
Photograph

Described aptly as 'the supreme triumph of Elizabethan architecture'. Hardwick, begun in 1590, is as much the culmination of Bess of Hardwick's building mania, as it is of Smythson's development in the art of effective massing. (J.H.)

18 MERTON COLLEGE, OXFORD
Photograph

The south side of Fellow's Quadrangle with its four-storeyed centrepiece built 1608–10. (J.H.)

19 COBHAM HALL, KENT
Photograph

The porch on the north wing built for William, Lord Cobham, and dated 1594. (J.H.)

20 CHARLTON HOUSE, GREENWICH, LONDON
Photograph

Although built for Sir Adam Newton, tutor to Henry, Prince of Wales, there is nothing in this house to reflect the Prince's Italianate court. The Dietterlinesque details of the frontispiece were carved about 1610. It is worth comparing this house with Houghton Conquest (196, 197). (J.H.)

21 AUDLEY END, ESSEX
Engraving by Henry Winstanley, *c.*1688
Photograph

This was the most stupendous of all Jacobean houses. Its 'Surveyor' may have been Bernart Janssen and it was built between 1603 and 1610 for that grandee, Thomas Howard, Earl of Suffolk. (J.H.)

22 BRAMSHILL HOUSE, HAMPSHIRE
Photograph

For a frontispiece, this is the culmination in Jacobean fantasy. It must have been planned about 1605 and its builder was Lord Zouche. (J.H.)

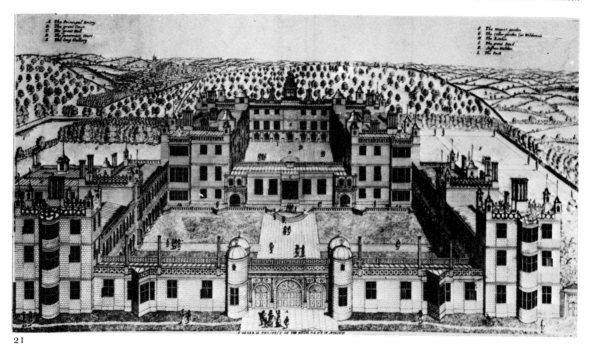

21

Robert Smythson (?1536–1614)
23 LONGLEAT HOUSE, WILTSHIRE
Design for a two-storeyed pilastered bay window
Pen and wash: 35·5 × 18·1
Royal Institute of British Architects

This may be Smythson's earliest design for the windows at Longleat, built by him and Allen Maynard 1572–79. It is also the first English architectural drawing to be presented in a recognizably Renaissance manner. (J.H.)

Robert Smythson (?1536–1614)
24 WORKSOP MANOR, NOTTINGHAMSHIRE
Design for the hall screen
Pen and wash: 25·7 × 33·6
Royal Institute of British Architects

Although not executed, this was intended for the house built by Smythson about 1583 for George Talbot, Earl of Shrewsbury who was the husband of the formidable Bess of Hardwick. Although no comparable collection of a late Elizabethan architect's drawings have survived, it is probably that Smythson's attention to the supervision of interior details was then uncommon. (J.H.)

Robert Smythson (?1536–1614)
25 DESIGN FOR AN UNIDENTIFIED COUNTRY HOUSE
Pen and wash: 32·7 × 47
Royal Institute of British Architects

This has been associated stylistically with both Wollaton Hall and Hardwick Hall.

23

25

It is the only complete elevation that has survived for a house and should be compared with Jones's designs of 1608 which likewise lack architectonic discipline. (J.H.)

Robert Smythson (?1536–1614)

26 DESIGN FOR A ROSE WINDOW
Pen: 34·2 × 8·6
Royal Institute of British Architects

Inscribed 'the Platte of a rounde: window: Standinge in A: Rounde: Walle: Anno: 1599'. This shows that Smythson's technical virtuosity was not acquired by rule of thumb alone. (J.H.)

The Jacobean Romantic:
Jones and Robert Cecil, Earl of Salisbury

In 1606, Edmund Bolton, then in Italy, inscribed in a book given to Jones the pregnant words that through him 'there is hope that sculpture, modelling, architecture, painting, acting and all that is praise-worthy in the elegant arts of the ancients, may one day find their way across the Alps into England'. The moment at which we can forecast Jones as a positive architect can be pin-pointed accurately by two precious designs both made in 1608: for the New Exchange, known as Britain's Burse, on The Strand (28) and for the completion of the central tower of old St Paul's Cathedral (30). Both were unexecuted, but both were produced under the patronage of Sir Robert Cecil, Earl of Salisbury, for whom Jones had designed entertainments at Salisbury House and Theobalds in July 1606, May 1607 and May 1608, and was to be again employed at the opening of Britain's Burse, April 10th, 1609. Cecil was probably not slow to recognize the latent Italianism of Jones in contrast to the traditional Office of Works' style of Simon Basil, the Surveyor. Indeed, Basil was Cecil's man, for he had been employed on Salisbury House in 1601; he seems consistently to have been sought for advice over the building of Hatfield from 1607, and in the same year probably employed for the enlargements to Cecil's Whitehall Lodging overlooking the Privy Garden (PRO E. 351. 3243). Cecil was probably too innured to the reactionary style of the late Elizabethan court to have had the confidence to execute Jones's Italianate dream-like design for the Exchange. What was built, again by Basil, was drawn (29) by John Smythson 1618–19. However inaccurate this rare topographical drawing may be, it is enough to suggest that whoever thought he might have been improving upon the other, and whatever may be recognized as Italianate elements in the composition, Cecil was, nevertheless, content with a compromising style. He may have been unwilling to put his trust in someone who was totally inexperienced in architecture, and he was probably right. The designs for the Exchange and St Paul's have the insubstantiality of theatre architecture. They are painterly, delicately-coloured drawings, re-created from the background of a masque. Authority for the elements so inconfidently composed can be found in the pages of Palladio, Serlio or from Sangallo's engraved designs for St Peters.

Simultaneously with all this activity, Cecil and his 'surveyors' were empirically making progress at Hatfield House, where the influence of the Exchange can be detected in the decision to give the inner court front to the south a pilastered façade over an open loggia. This was Robert Liming's design made in October 1609. But it was never executed, for the whole of this front had been designed anew by April 1610. The result may be Jones's first architectural achievement and it is one that has never been convincingly associated with an entry in the Hatfield building accounts for February 28th, 1610: 'To Inigo Jones, as your ho: reward given him for drawinge of some Architecture 10–0–0'. This sum of money points to a substantial task, for a little over a year earlier, Jones had only received £13 6s 8d for the whole designing of the entertainment to celebrate the opening of the Exchange on April 10th, 1609.

Like the Exchange, the south front of Hatfield House shows indecision and an ambivalence between a pure Franco-Italianate idiom (Jones visited Paris in 1609) and the conservative ornamental style of Basil Liming. The most classical parts are the windows and the clock tower. This latter dominates the front and must have been conceived as an integral part of the general visual effect. It is markedly simple and classical, more so than can be credited to Basil. If the classical parts of Hatfield are by Jones, then here may be his first executed architectural work. In the year that intervenes between the new Exchange and St Paul's and Hatfield, his design has progressed from something insubstantial to a more lasting expression of architectural manners.

In a church in Shropshire, however, the masque prop was transformed into alabaster, in a strangely naïve, crudely-carved tomb for which a design exists in Jones's hand. This is the monument (33, 34) in St Chad's, Norton-in-Hales, Shropshire, to Sir Rowland Cotton, and his wife who died in childbed in 1606. The sarcophagus appears in the scene the Fallen House of Chivalry, from Prince Henry's *Barriers*, January 6th, 1610 (59), and the balls on columns are in a design for a scene for the masque of *Oberon*, January 1st, 1611 (61–65). No Jonesian survival is as evocative as this; nothing is so redolent of this early period of Jones's life. Jones is here the Jacobean romantic. (J.H.)

28

John de Critz (d.1642)

27 ROBERT CECIL, 1ST EARL OF SALISBURY 1563–1612
Oil on panel: 90·2 × 73·4; dated 1602
The National Portrait Gallery (107)

28 THE NEW EXCHANGE OR BRITAIN'S BURSE IN THE STRAND
Design for the front elevation
Pen, pencil and watercolour: 48·3 × 73
The Provost and Fellows of Worcester College

In 1608 when Cecil acquired a strip of land fronting the Strand and belonging to Durham House, Simon Basil built the Exchange as drawn by Smythson when he visited London 1618–19. It will never be known if Jones's design is an improvement on Basil's, or if Basil's building is a late Elizabethan interpretation of Jones's more Italianate essay. One would have had more admiration for Jones had it not been for the ludicrously improbable towers. Some eclectic engraved sources and a reading of book four of Serlio provides basis of Jones's design. (J.H.)

Robert Smythson (?1536–1614)
29 NEW EXCHANGE *c.*1609
Half elevation of the front
Pen: 52 × 26
Royal Institute of British Architects

This survey drawing accompanies a plan. Although its accuracy has been questioned, it is, nevertheless, a fairly faithful representation of the Exchange as seen by Smythson, when he came to London to view the latest fashions. (J.H.)

30   31

30 OLD ST PAUL'S CATHEDRAL
Design for the completion of the central tower
Pen, pencil and watercolour: 75 × 51·5
The Provost and Fellows of Worcester College

In July 1608 James I asked the Lord Mayor and the Bishop of London to initiate a commission to have the old medieval cathedral surveyed and a new spire built. Robert Cecil was a member of this commission. The estimate, presumably from Jones, was for £22,527 2s 3d, but nothing was proceeded with. (J.H.)

31 HATFIELD HOUSE, HERTFORDSHIRE
The south front of the court and the clock tower
Photograph

Here is the front as re-designed by April 1610, on the basis of a revision of Robert Liming's design submitted in October 1609. A comparison with the New Exchange design made a year earlier is instructive. The most classical parts of Hatfield are the clock tower, which is unique for its date, and the windows with their sills supported by three consoles – significantly of a type that first appears, if judged by Smythson, at the New Exchange. (J.H.)

Entertainment at Salisbury House, between May 6th and 11th, 1608

32 A ROCK AND AN ARCHWAY
Pen and brown ink: 23·6 × 33·4 O&S 13; S&B 15
The Trustees of the Chatsworth Settlement

Inigo Jones and Ben Jonson were employed four times to provide spectacles in honour of James I and his Queen, Anne of Denmark. They were as follows:
(1) July 24th, 1606. Entertainment at Theobalds on the occasion of the visit of Christian IV of Denmark. The Hatfield accounts record the payment of £23 'To

32

Inigo Jones the painter for his Chardges and paines'. Jonson wrote the text. Christiar
IV arrived in England on July 17th and rode, with James I, to Theobalds on the 24th
where Salisbury 'for four days together, feasted them and all their trains according to
their estates and dignities shewing them many signs of love, duty, and heartie
welcome'. The entertainment took the form of the Three Hours, Law, Justice and
Peace welcoming the Kings. These were placed, seated on clouds, over the entrance
porch in the inner courtyard. The Kings were addressed in both Latin and English
and the walls were inscribed with Latin epigrams.

(2) May 22nd, 1607. Entertainment on the occasion of Salisbury handing over Theobalds to James I. No payments to Jones survive in the Cecil Papers but this must surely
be his work and again in collaboration with Jonson. Theobalds was handed over to
James I in exchange for the palace of Hatfield, where Cecil was to build a stupendous
new house and give Jones his earliest opportunity to express himself in building (31).
The entertainment took place in the Long Gallery, possibly darkened, as the impact
of the spectacle depended on the manipulation of light. On arriving a white curtain
was withdrawn to reveal 'a gloomy obscure place'. Mercury descended in a flying
posture to tell the mourning Genius of the house of her new master. The black vanished
revealing the Lararium, the seat of the household gods, with the Three Fates in
tableau in a grotto. The Lararium was elaborately lit with coloured lights achieved
by placing candles behind glasses filled with coloured water.

(3) Between May 6th and 11th, 1608. Entertainment at Salisbury House presumably

33   34

in celebration of Cecil's appointment as Treasurer that month. No text by Jonson survives, although like Jones he received £20 for his labours. The accounts record the characters and the nature of the decor. It was staged in the library of Salisbury House and the characters included a Conjuror, Fancy, Barahon and Eight Spirits. There were curtains, presumably withdrawn as in the 1607 Theobalds fête, and a rock lit by candles set behind glasses containing coloured liquid to create lighting effects. Two sketches (32) show the rock and also an archway, possibly at the foot of a staircase.

(4) April 10th, 1609. Entertainment on the occasion of the opening of Britain's Burse. The text does not survive but costs came to £179 in all and the form it took was one typical of late Elizabethan receptions in honour of the Queen: a grumbling keeper of the new exchange eventually reveals himself as a prosperous merchant and presents gifts to the royal family. Other characters were Genius, Mercury and Lachesis. (R.S.)

33 MONUMENT TO SIR ROWLAND AND LADY COTTON, ST. CHAD'S CHURCH, NORTON-IN-HALES, SHROPSHIRE
Photograph

34 DESIGN FOR THE MONUMENT TO SIR ROWLAND AND LADY COTTON, ST CHAD'S, NORTON-IN-HALES, SHROPSHIRE
Pen and wash: 26 × 20
Royal Institute of British Architects

The monument as executed is basically as designed here, with divergencies probably due to the sculptor, but at a later date the monument was adapted to take the effigy of Sir Rowland who died in 1634. His wife had died in childbed November 23rd,

1606. As there is such a close comparison to effects in Prince Henry's Barriers of January 1610 (59, 60) and the Masque of *Oberon* of January 1611, a date around this time is probable. Dr John Newman, who has published this design, has demonstrated that Rowland Cotton, born about 1577, was probably attached to the court of Henry Prince of Wales, for Henry is constantly called Cotton's 'master'. In Thomas Coryate's *Crudities* of 1611, dedicated to the Prince, the tenth panegyric is by Cotton. Dr Newman has also shown that Cotton was a patron of biblical scholarship. The Cotton design came from the collection of John and William Talman and probably became detached from the Jones–Webb collection and sold in one of John's many sales. (J.H.)

Jones and Anne of Denmark, 1605–11

The Early Masques and Entertainments

Though court masques had flourished in England for more than a century, the form was revitalized for the Stuart court by the work of Inigo Jones and Ben Jonson. Despite their famous quarrel, this extraordinary collaboration continued for over twenty-five years, and produced the most serious and sophisticated court spectacles England had ever seen. Masques were essential to the life of the Renaissance court; their allegories gave a higher meaning to the realities of politics and power, their idealized fictions created heroic roles for the leaders of society. To the age of James I and Charles I, appearing in a masque was not merely playing a part. It was, in a profound sense, precisely the opposite: when Jones and Jonson presented Queen Anne as Bel-Anna, Queen of the Ocean, or King James as Pan, the universal god, or Prince Henry as Oberon, Prince of Faery, a deep truth about the monarchy was realized and embodied in action, and the monarchs were revealed in roles that expressed the strongest Renaissance beliefs about the nature of kingship, the obligations and perquisites of royalty

Jones's first masques were commissioned by Queen Anne for herself and her ladies to dance in. For these productions the architect designed a stage that was utterly new to England, employing complex machinery, elaborate lighting effects, and illusionistic settings devised according to the rules of perspective. An artificial sea with great sea-beasts and mermaids astonished the audience of Jones's and Jonson's first masque, *The Masque of Blackness*, in 1605. In the next year, for Jonson's *Hymenaei*, Jones created a gigantic globe of gold and silver seemingly floating in mid-air, which turned to reveal the masquers seated in 'a mine of light'. In 1609 Jonson's *The Masque of Queens* opened on a hell scene, complete with fire and smoke; this was made to vanish in an instant, to be replaced by 'a glorious and magnificent building figuring the House of Fame ... filled with several-coloured lights like emeralds, rubies, sapphires, carbuncles, etc'.

But masques were not merely theatrical spectacles. The form was so deeply involved with the protocol of the court and the aristocratic hierarchy that to devise a suitable fiction in itself posed considerable problems. For the season of 1605 the Queen had asked Jones and Jonson to create a masque in which she and her ladies could appear in blackface. If Jonson found the commission an awkward one, his ingenuity and learning were equal to it. On Twelfth Night the court saw *The Masque of Blackness*, a Neo-platonic allegory about the power of kingship, in which the black nymphs of Niger are bleached by the 'sciential' light of the monarch of the white realm of Albion. The complexities of all this, moreover, could not be expressed by the masquers themselves.

Masquers are not actors; a lady or gentleman participating in a masque remains a lady or gentleman, and is not relieved from observing all the niceties of behaviour at court. Queen Anne and her ladies danced in the masque because dancing is the perquisite of every lady and gentleman. It was, however, unthinkable for the Queen to become an actress and play a part. For speaking roles, therefore, professional actors had to be used, and this meant that the form was by nature divided between players and masquers, actors and dancers. In the hands of Jonson and Jones, this practical

35   37

consideration became a metaphysical conceit, and the form as they developed it rapidly separated into two sections. The first, called the anti-masque, was performed by professionals, and regularly presented a world of disorder or vice, everything that the ideal world of the courtly masquers was to overcome and supersede. When the moment of transformation arrived, the dancers in their splendid costumes descended from the stage and moved the heroic fiction into the court itself. They danced before the King, and then, merging the ideal world with the real, took partners from the audience, concluding the theatrical performance with a grand ball. Poetry and spectacle thus culminated in the shared pleasures of an aristocratic community, and the dancing often continued for most of the night. (s.o.)

The Visit to France, 1609

Jones visited France in the summer of 1609. A warrant dated June 16th authorizes the payment to him of £13 6s 8d for carrying 'letters for his Majesty's service into France'. The visit must have taken place after the performance of *The Masque of Queens* on February 2nd and was, therefore, of short duration. However short, it would have given Jones the opportunity to study at first hand French mannerist architecture by du Cerçeau and de l'Orme. The use of Jones as a messenger was probably a convenient means of enabling him to assimilate the taste of the French court, particularly the Valois. In 1632 Jones used *Le Balet Comique de la Reyne*, 1581, the climax of Valois festival art, as a basis for his masque *Tempe Restored* (315–318). He would also have seen the Place Royale, and the Place Dauphine, sources for his future Covent Garden development. (R.S.)

Isaac Oliver (d.1617)

35 ANNE OF DENMARK
Miniature: 5·2 × 4·3
Her Majesty The Queen

Anne is wearing an elaborate head-dress of the type Jones designed for her masque appearances. Jones always seems to have executed special studies of the Queen's head-dresses and three survive, for *The Masque of Queens* (1609), *Tethy's Festival* (1610) and probably for *Love Freed from Ignorance and Folly* (1611). None tallies with that in Oliver's miniature (R.S.)

By or after John de Critz (d.1642)

36 ANNE OF DENMARK, *c.*1605
Oil on panel: 63·5 × 50·75
Ipswich Museums

The portrait depicts Anne as she looked during the period when she danced in *The Masque of Blackness* (1605). This is the earliest portrait type of the Queen to gain currency in the new reign. (R.S.)

Attributed to Abraham Blyenberch (*fl. c.*1621)

37 BEN JONSON (?1573–1637)
Oil on canvas: 47 × 41·9
The National Portrait Gallery

38 Ben Jonson, *The Characters of two Royal Masques, the one of Blackness, the other of Beauty.*
London, 1608. Presentation copy from the author to Queen Anne of Denmark
The British Museum

The published texts of Jonson's early masques, from *The Masque of Blackness* through *Oberon the Fairy Prince*, reveal much about the seriousness with which the poet treated this ephemeral form. Scrupulously researched and annotated in detail, they seem to insist in the most literal way on the authority of poetry, the reality of fictions. The spectacular visions of Jones's scenic displays are in fact elaborate symbols expressing arcane meanings, and the glosses of Jonson's printed texts provide the key. After wonder, for the Renaissance audience, came understanding. (s.o.)

39 MASQUER: A DAUGHTER OF NIGER
Watercolour, mostly opaque, heightened with gold and silver, now tarnished:
29 × 15·9 O&S 1; S&B 1
The Trustees of the Chatsworth Settlement

40 A TORCHBEARER: AN OCEANIA
Watercolour, heightened with silver, now tarnished, and gold: 28·5 × 18·7 O&S 4;
S&B 4

The Masque of Blackness was Jonson's and Jones's first court masque. It was led by Anne of Denmark, attended by eleven other aristocratic ladies who, as black-faced Daughters of Niger (39), journey to Britannia, an island ruled by a Sun 'whose beams shine day and night, and of force, To blanch an Ethiop . . .'. The performance opened with a curtain painted with a hunt, which fell to reveal a seascape over which, on an upper stage, presided the Moon on a silver throne amidst the clouds. A sea with moving waves was contrived, in which were musicians as tritons and mermaids backed, by a vista of ocean 'drawn by the lines of perspective, the whole work shooting downwards from the eye; which decorum made it more conspicuous, and caught the eye afar off with a wandering beauty'. The masquers made their entrance and exit, probably presupposing a proscenium arch, in an elaborately lit shell of mother-of-pearl drawn by sea monsters.

37

41   42

Visually the production was revolutionary in its use of single-point perspective, but it was only revolutionary to those qualified to read the scene correctly and this was to take Jones many years to achieve. The Venetian ambassador alone was probably qualified to understand it and he thought it 'very beautiful and sumptuous'. Dudley Carleton, in contrast, saw it as separate elements within the tradition of Elizabethan entertainments. He refers to it as a 'Pagent' with 'all fish and no water'. The blacking of the ladies faces was an 'ugly sight' and their costumes 'Curtizan-like'. (R.S.)

Unknown Masque, *c.*1605

41 WINGED MASQUER
Watercolour, mostly opaque, heightened with gold and silver, now tarnished: 27·6 × 18 O&S 5; S&B 418
The Trustees of the Chatsworth Settlement

This drawing possibly precedes even those for *The Masque of Blackness* in date. It is definitely for a masquer with the ankle-length dress for dancing and may conceivably relate to a masque given by Anne of Denmark to welcome Prince Henry at Winchester in the autumn of 1603. Whatever it relates to, it is early in date and feeble in execution. Jones was over thirty and clearly learning to draw based on a tradition epitomized by John White's costume studies (81). The type of masquing dress is directly within the late Elizabethan tradition (82). (R.S.)

Ben Jonson, *Hymenaei*, 5 January 1606
Attributed to John de Critz (d.1642)

42 CALLED LUCY HARINGTON, COUNTESS OF BEDFORD
Oil on canvas: 198 × 106·7
Trustees of the late Earl of Berkeley

Hymenaei was staged to celebrate the wedding of the Earl of Essex to Frances Howard, daughter of the Earl of Suffolk. In it Jonson uses the alliance as a vehicle to glorify the 'marriage' effected by James I in the creation of Great Britain and for a pyrotechnic display of learning about nuptial rituals in antiquity. The masque opened with a Roman marriage ceremony centering on an altar, and went on to achieve scene-change for the first time by the device of a turning machine, a *machina versatilis*. A globe of the earth revolved to reveal a microcosm, from which stepped forth eight masquer lords as humours and affections. As in *The Masque of Blackness* there was an upper stage tableau revealed, this time of Juno enthroned, and, for the first time, clouds descended sloping gently to the ground bearing the ladies as 'The Powers of Juno'. At the close of the masque the scene was 'all covered with clouds, as night' as it had been at the beginning.

No designs by Jones survive for this important masque with its significant developments in the use of machinery. Three paintings (others at Woburn Abbey and Welbeck Abbey) depict lady masquers in their costumes provide a unique record of what the dresses actually looked like. What the artist saw and we in fact see is a Jacobean lady wearing a fanciful extension of court dress with a skirt shortened for dancing. Jonson describes the costumes as 'the most true impression of a celestial figure'. (R.S.)

43 BEN JONSON, *The Masque of Queens*, 1609
Manuscript
Photograph

The Masque of Queens was the most famous and spectacular of Jonson's early masques; it displays not only remarkable poetic and dramatic intensity, but also an enormous range of scholarly erudition. The witches of its anti-masque were created out of a wide variety of authorities on demonology; its queens based firmly on the accounts of ancient and modern historians. At the command of the fourteen-year-old Prince Henry, Jonson prepared an extensively annotated text, which was printed both in quarto in 1609 and in the folio of 1616. The Prince himself received a presentation copy written in Jonson's own hand, with a special dedication "To the glorie of our owne, and greefe of other Nations: My Lord Henry Prince of great Britayne'. (S.O.)

44 SCENE 2: THE HOUSE OF FAME
Pen and black ink washed with grey: 27·8 × 19·9 O&S 15; S&B 14
The Trustees of the Chatsworth Settlement

45 DIAGRAM OF THE HOUSE OF FAME
Photograph

46 MASQUER QUEEN: CAMILLA
Pen and black ink washed with warm grey: 28·3 × 17·2 O&S 17; S&B 19
The Trustees of the Chatsworth Settlement

44

47 MASQUER QUEEN: BERENICE
Pen and black ink washed with greenish grey: 29·7 × 18 O&S 22; S&B 24
The Trustees of the Chatsworth Settlement

48 HEAD-DRESS FOR ANNE OF DENMARK: BEL-ANNA, QUEEN OF THE OCEAN
Pen and brown ink: 18·4 × 13 O&S 29; S&B 422
The Trustees of the Chatsworth Settlement

The Masque of Queens represented a decided development within the masque as a form by the introduction of an anti-masque as a foil to the main one. This had its own setting of 'an ugly hell' with the anti-masquers as witches who were banished 'scarce suffering the memory of such a thing' revealing the House of Fame (44) with the masquers sitting in tableau above. Anne and her ladies were eleven virtuous queens (46, 47) led by Bel-Anna, Queen of the Ocean (48) who combined the virtues of them all. The elaborately lit pyramid on which they sat was a *machina versatilis*, which revolved to reveal Fame on the other side, allowing the Queens to descend and make a triumphal entry in chariots through the doors at stage level.

This was the most complicated setting to date. In form the House of Fame relates to pageant arches of the type erected for James I's Coronation Entry (12) and the use of coloured lights, 'like emeralds, rubies, sapphires, carbuncles, etc' is an effect repeated throughout the early masques. The drawing for the House of Fame in *The Masque of Queens* (44) is the earliest one we have for a stage-setting by Jones. It shows the masquers in tableau on their machine for which the Works Accounts record the

46   50

payment for a 'great piller with diverse wheeles and devices for moving rounde thereof'. Musicians seem to be on the roof of the building and it is encompassed by the earliest sketch of a proscenium arch. Below Jones sketches Fame, who rode on the opposite side of the *machina versatilis*.

Jonson acknowledges Jones for the attire of the witches and 'the invention and architecture of the whole scene and machine'. He also gives a rare glimpse into Jones's role as artistic director of the production. Jonson admits that Jones supervised 'the going about of the chariots' and 'the binding of the witches'. (R.S.)

49 Samuel Daniel, *Tethys' Festival*, London 1610
The British Museum

50 TETHYS OR A NYMPH
Pen and brown ink washed with brown: 33·5 × 17·8 O&S 54; S&B 38
The Trustees of the Chatsworth Settlement

Tethys' Festival was staged on June 5th, 1610, in honour of the creation of Henry as Prince of Wales and was led by Anne of Denmark as Tethys with her ladies as rivers. No scenery designs survive, but it opened with a port scene in perspective with ships moving to and fro. This was taken away, while moving lights held the spectators' attention, to reveal the Queen and her river nymphs enthroned in a shell grotto of silver and gold with the usual coloured lights 'like diamonds, rubies, sapphires, emeralds, and sucklike'. There was, for the first time, a third scene for the masquers

51

return to the grotto 'and suddenly vanish'. The latter 'in the form of a half round' was a *machina versatilis*, which revolved at the end changing to 'a most pleasant and artificial grove'. Campion directly quotes Inigo Jones's own words in describing the scene 'in the language of the architector who contrived it' which included pillars of 'modern architecture'. (R.S.)

Ben Jonson, *Love Freed from Ignorance and Folly*, February 3rd, 1611

51 SCENE 2: THE RELEASE OF THE DAUGHTERS OF THE MORN
Pen and brown ink washed with brown: 46.8 × 38.8 O&S 74; S&B 17
The Trustees of the Chatsworth Settlement

Love Freed from Ignorance and Folly was originally planned for 1610 but was not performed until the next year. After the stupendous spectacles of the *Barriers* and *Tethys' Festival*, *Love Freed from Ignorance and Folly* was one of Anne's least costly masques. Jonson's text is reticent as to scenic spectacle but Jones's design (51) is a repetition of the arrangement of *The Masque of Queens* (44). The masque opened with a dialogue between Love and a Sphinx before a cliff, followed by an anti-masque of Follies. The cliff was possibly a *scena ductilis* drawn off to reveal the Prison of Night, presumably with clouds drawn over the upper stage. These parted to reveal Anne and her ladies as the Daughters of the Morn seated in three groups, each a *machina versatilis*. They had the customary elaborate lighting and presumably the seats revolved to allow the masquers to descend and make their entry through the door beneath at stage level. Few designs evoke so forcefully the duality of Jones's visual inspiration: above there is a cloud vision on the lines of those in the celebrated Florentine *intermezzi* of 1589, which Jones could have known from the engravings by Agostino Carracci and Epifanio d'Arfiano, below there is a castle gate in the vein of Elizabethan and Jacobean Neo-gothic architecture. (R.S.)

In the service of Henry, Prince of Wales: 1610–12

Surveyor to the Prince

Jones's first documented contact with Prince Henry occurs in January 1610, when he designed the masque for Prince Henry's *Barriers*. Thomas Howard, 2nd Earl of Arundel and Surrey, then aged twenty-five, was one of the Prince's supporters and seems to have been frequently attending the Prince since 1607. Through this, Jones must have become a member of the Arundel circle. The Prince, who had acquired the Nonsuch library in 1609 and was well known 'to valew none but extraordinary persons', must have been impressed by the Italianism of Jones. Certainly by May 1610 'Mr Inico Joanes', as his Surveyor, headed a list of establishment that included Robert Peake as 'picture maker'. For Jones the future must have seemed auspicious and his pay began from January 1611. The scene was set for great things. But they were not to be, for it would appear that Jones may have lost the Prince's favours long before that tragic death on November 6th, 1612. Unfortunately no architectural work documented for Henry's brief tenure as Prince of Wales can be supported by drawings or topographical views. It is not known if Jones was responsible for any of the £1586 spent on St James's Palace. As Prince Henry's Surveyor, he must have been regarded as capable of architectural design. Yet by 1611 a French garden designer, Salomon de Caus, had been sent over by the French Ambassador for the Prince's water works at Richmond, and on June 15th, 1611 a Medicean architect from Florence had been summoned to make designs for 'fountains, summer-houses, galleries and other things on a site in which his Highness is most interested' – almost certainly for Richmond. This was the mysterious Constantino de Servi (he also painted a portrait of the Prince and a life-size picture of his favourite horse), who may well have been far more versed in sophisticated Italianate design than Jones. Supplanting even de Caus, he was obviously creating a fabulous garden at Richmond, with a 'great figure . . . three times as large as the one at Pratolino, with rooms inside, a dove-cot in the head and grottoes in the base', and so great was his success with the Prince that from March 1612 he received an annuity of £200. Had the Prince lived, an Italian Surveyor of the Works might have changed the course of Jones's career. However, the friendship between Prince Charles, Lord Arundel and Jones was a portent for a safe voyage. (J.H.)

52 Serlio, *Booke of Architecture*, 1611
Translated from Italian into Dutch, from Dutch into English by Robert Peake, printed by Simon Stafford 1611.
Royal Institute of British Architects

54

This is the only complete English edition of Serlio and was the first complete treatise on architecture in the English language. Although by 1611 an English edition of Serlio, one of the most used books by the late Elizabethans and early Jacobeans, must have seemed a great necessity, Peake's dedication to Henry, Prince of Wales is probably a pointer to his awareness of the Prince's role as a patron of the arts of Italianate design. We should perhaps also remember that Jones, Peake and de Servi shared Court positions as painters. (J.H.)

53 Salomon de Caus, *La Perspective, avec La Raison des Ombres et Miroirs*, London 1612
The British Museum

54 Salomon de Caus, *Les Raisons des Forces Mouvantes avec diverses Machines*, Frankfurt 1615
The British Museum

55 Salomon de Caus, *La Pratique et Demonstration des Horloges Solaires*, Paris 1624
The British Museum

56 Salomon de Caus, *Institution Harmonique Diversée en deux Parties*, Frankfurt 1615
Collection of Mr. John Harris

It is not clear when de Caus (1576–1626) came to England. His first association may have been with Queen Anne, for in 1607–8 he was laying out the gardens to her Lodging at Greenwich. After this he may have returned to France, for he was brought from France again to advise Prince Henry on the gardens at Richmond. His relationship with de Servi is not clear, and indeed de Servi may have claimed credit for work at Richmond that had been designed by de Caus. In the second part of de Caus's *Les Raisons des Forces Mouvantes . . . ou sont desseynees plusier Grotes & Fontaines*, published in France in 1624, but written from Heidelberg, he engraved his fantastic Italianate gardens in the style of Pratolino and Bomarzo. In 1611 de Caus had been summoned to Hatfield House by Robert Cecil to lay out new waterworks; and in 1613, or soon after, the Princess Elizabeth and Frederick V, Elector Palatine of the Rhine, brought him to lay out the elaborate gardens at Heidelberg. De Caus was no ordinary gardener. His *Institution Harmonique*, dedicated to Queen Anne of Denmark, shows that he was a Neo-platonist, and *La Pratique et Demonstration des Horloges Solaries* places him in the company of mathematicians and empirical scientists. It was probably through his contacts with the Prince of Wales and Jones that his son or nephew, Isaac de Caus, (349, 363–65) came to play such an important supporting role in the execution of many of Jones's buildings and the laying out of their gardens. (J.H.)

The Prince's Festivals

Prince Henry was a considerable patron of the arts, and like his mother, an avid masquer. He was also an enthusiastic horseman, and loved such martial fêtes as tilts and barriers. Romantic and scholarly by nature, the young prince employed Inigo Jones as his Surveyor, though what particular projects this position entailed are not known. He also commissioned Jones and Jonson to restore to life the world of ancient chivalry in a series of entertainments with himself as the central figure. The character he took was from the Arthurian legends, Meliadus, Lord of the Isles, the lover of the Lady of the Lake. As Meliadus, he tilted in the *Barriers* of 1610 to celebrate his investiture as Prince of Wales. In Jonson's fiction, Meliadus and his knights are summoned by Merlin and King Arthur to revive British knighthood. Jones's settings for this production are a precise expression of the Prince's mind; the ruins of the House of Chivalry are miraculously metamorphosed into the elegant, romantically medieval pavilion of St George's Portico.

In the Christmas masque of the next year, Jones and Jonson presented the Prince as Oberon, son of King Arthur and heir to the kingdom of Faery. In this exquisite work, Spenserian romance joins with classical mythology to create a Britain which unites the traditions of chivalry with Roman order. In the development of Jones's stage, the production was a crucial one. The architect first designed the work around a *machina versatilis*, or turning machine. This was a two-sided setting that revolved on a pivot; Jones had already used it for the great globe in *Hymenaei* and the House of Fame in *The Masque of Queens*. This was a spectacular device, but for a progression of scenes as complex as that required by *Oberon, The Fairy Prince*, the machine lacked flexibility. So Jones re-designed the masque with quite different stage mechanics. He now employed the *scena ductilis*, or tractable scene, consisting of a series of flats set in grooves in the stage, which could be swiftly and quietly drawn aside to reveal the setting behind them. Since with this device the number of scene changes was limited only by the number of grooves the stage could contain, the flexibility of Jones's theatre became, for all practical purposes, infinite. From *Oberon, The Fairy Prince* forward, the *scena ductilis* remained Jones's basic scenic machine.

Jones's costume for Oberon shows King James's heir as medieval knight and Roman emperor combined, and reveals much about the age's hopes for this young man. The King, for all his scholarly virtues and pacific policies, was awkward and without charm. Prince Henry's sudden death in 1612, at the age of eighteen, deprived the nation's poets and artists not only of a patron, but of a romantic hero as well. (S.O.)

57

Isaac Oliver (d.1617)
57 HENRY PRINCE OF WALES, *c*.1610
Miniature: 5·1 × 4
The Fitzwilliam Museum, Cambridge

Oliver was extensively patronized by the young prince. This miniature, of which a number of versions are recorded (e.g. National Portrait Gallery and in the Mauritshuis, The Hague) depicts the Prince *à l'antique* in profile against a shell niche. It should be compared with Jones's presentation of him in antique attire in *Oberon, The Fairy Prince* (65). (R.S.)

Attributed to Isaac Oliver (d.1617)
58 HENRY, PRINCE OF WALES, *c*.1610
Oil on canvas: 228·6 × 218·4
The Parham Park Collection

This is the most important known large-scale portrait of Prince Henry and reflects accurately the heir apparent's preoccupation with his own official image. As in the spectacles, devised by Jonson and Jones, Henry is presented as embodying both the knightly virtues of the past and the ideals of the present. He is depicted as a knight in armour, his bases embroidered with an obscure *impresa* with allusions to the Arthurian Legend, the hand arising from the lake bearing not the sword but the anchor of Hope while a sun arises in the distance. The portrait formula, however, is that of the classical triumphal equestrian image with its imperial overtones.

During the period that this was painted Isaac Oliver was paid by the Prince for several large-scale paintings, including 'one great Picture'. Constantino de Servi is recorded as having painted a whole length of the Prince and of his horse but not

46

60

apparently together. Henry's search for a portrait painter led him to open up negotiations with Miereveldt in an effort to induce him to England. (R.S.)

Prince Henry's *The Barriers*, January 6th, 1610

59 SCENE I: THE FALLEN HOUSE OF CHIVALRY
Pen and brown ink washed with brown: 24·5 × 27 O&S 36; S&B 194
The Trustees of the Chatsworth Settlement

60 SCENE II: ST GEORGE'S PORTICO
Pen and brown ink washed with brown: 26·5 × 32·4 O&S 37; S&B 195
The Trustees of the Chatsworth Settlement

The Barriers of 1610 was Jones's first significant task for Prince Henry. Staged on Twelfth Night 1610, before the assembled court, they were designed to present the heir apparent not only as the epitome of the knightly virtues, the new Arthurian-British hero, but as the Renaissance Maecenas. Ben Jonson and Inigo Jones, both in word and visual image, created a rich tissue of allusion around this first public appearance of the young, adulated prince. The vehicle was the knightly diversion of the barriers, usually presented with scattered décor within the late Elizabethan tradition

62

64

but, as in the masque, Jones deliberately superimposed on to this straggling form of court entertainment the rules of single point perspective. The opening scene or shutter depicted the ruined House of Chivalry. King Arthur appeared in the heavens to present the Prince in his role as Meliadus (*Miles-a-Deo*) with a symbolic shield and the scene then changed to St George's Portico, Lady Chivalry awakening from her slumber to hail the advent of her new champion.

The designs capture the dichotomy in the prince's official persona, the ruins are not only classical, a Trajan's column or the Coliseum derived from engravings, but also medieval. As in the case of the masque of *Oberon*, Jones, and along with him Jonson in his text, is trying to naturalise the new classical ideals over existing traditions of courtly chivalry: they succeed in an attempt to knit together a revival of chivalrous values with the re-introduction of classical architecture, which they believed had once existed in Britain:

More truth of architecture there was blazed
Than lived in all the ignorant Goths have razed.
There porticos were built, and seats for knights
That watched for all adventures, days and nights:
The niches filled with statues to invite
Young valours forth by their old forms to fight,
With arcs triumphal for their actions done . . .

The Prince was assisted by six challengers and there were fifty-six defendants. The spectacle began at 10 pm on the Saturday and lasted until Sunday morning. Jonson and Jones each received £40 and the total cost was about £2,500. (R.S.)

Ben Jonson, *Oberon, The Fairy Prince*, January 1st, 1611

61 PROJECT: SCENE OF ROCKS
Pen and brown ink washed with warm grey, prolongations of the scene on both sides sketched in black lead: 38·2 × 43·8 O&S 60; S&B 40
The Trustees of the Chatsworth Settlement

48

63

62 PROJECT: PALACE WITHIN A CAVERN
Pen and brown ink washed with warm grey, the architecture inscribed with incised lines: 36·5 × 40·5 O&S 61; S&B 44
The Trustees of the Chatsworth Settlement

63 PROJECT: INTERIOR OF THE PALACE WITHIN THE MACHINA VERSATILIS
Pen and brown ink washed with grey: 47 × 38·8 O&S 62; S&B 45
The Trustees of the Chatsworth Settlement

64 SCENE II: OBERON'S PALACE
Pen and light brown ink washed with grey and reinforced with pen and black ink, traces of former squaring-up: 33·3 × 39·3 O&S 62; S&B 42
The Trustees of the Chatsworth Settlement

65

65 OBERON

Pen and brown ink washed with grey: 29·2 × 14·9 O&S 70; S&B 52
The Trustees of the Chatsworth Settlement

The year after the *Barriers*, Jonson and Jones were called upon for a second time to
provide a vehicle for the Prince's appearance during the Christmas Revels of 1610–11.
It is possible that this project began as one for a *Barriers* on the lines of that of the
previous year but it was later reworked for the masque text we know by Jonson. Three
drawings connect with the early project and show Jones using his earliest scenic device
of a turning machine, a *machina versatilis*, an outcrop of rock (60) revolving to reveal
a palace in the classical style with a corridor leading back, as in St George's Portico
in the *Barriers*. The Palace revealed is a compilation based on a design for a church
in Serlio, with a stag and baying dogs on the pediment copied from the gateway to
the Château d'Anet, but probably derived from the engraving in du Cerçeau's book.

Whatever led to the abandonment of this project, the masque of *Oberon, The Fairy
Prince* as it was performed, utilized properly for the first time the shutter technique, the
so-called *scena ductilis*, a method which was infinitely flexible allowing any number of
scene changes as back-shutters were pushed forward or withdrawn along supporting
grooves. Not only did the spectacle strike the Venetian ambassador as 'very beautiful

68

throughout' but an English onlooker describes how 'the rock opened discovering a great throne with countless lights and colours all shifting, a lovely thing to see'. Once more the prince was cast in the role of Arthur's heir but with the addition, this time, of the title the 'Fairy Prince', thus gathering to himself the threads of Elizabethan royalist fairy mythology. As in the *Barriers* there is an architectural progression from rude rocks to the revelation of the Prince himself in a palace part Neo-gothic and part classical. Henry himself was dressed as a Roman emperor. (R.S.)

Designs for Tournaments, *c*.1610–1613

66 CAVE AND MOUNT
Pen and brown ink washed with brown: 29·6 × 19·5 O&S 46; S&B 404
The Trustees of the Chatsworth Settlement

67 HORSE CAPARISON
Pen and brown ink washed with brown: 26·2 × 21·8 O&S 47; S&B 465
The Trustees of the Chatsworth Settlement

68 ELEPHANT PAGEANT FOR RICHARD PRESTON, LORD DINGWALL, 1610
Pen and brown ink washed with brown: 29 × 20·6 O&S 45; S&B 464
The Trustees of the Chatsworth Settlement

Chivalrous spectacles were as frequent as masques at the Jacobean court. James I inherited his predecessors' custom of a tournament in the tiltyard of Whitehall Palace on his Accession Day, March 24th. These finally ceased in 1622, the result of a gradual decline, but under Prince Henry chivalrous exercises underwent a remarkable revival led by the Prince himself. Jones was commissioned to design decor in the form of pageant parade elephants or caverns hung with emblematic shields besides costumes for the knights and their attendants. The Elephant Pageant (68) was designed for Lord Dingwall for Accession Day 1610 and based by Jones on an elephant in an engraving of a battle scene by Cornelis Cort. It caused a sensation in the tilt-yard as it was so cumbrous in construction that it held up the progress of the tournament, while it crept around the tilt-yard. A spectacular tilt was also held on June 6th of that year as part of the fête to celebrate Henry's formal investiture as Prince of Wales. The main feature of that spectacle was the marvellous horse-caparisons 'Imbroydered with Pearls, Gould, and Silver, the like rich habiliaments for horses were never seene beefore'. (R.S.)

69 Thomas Coryate, *Crudities*, London, 1611
Presentation copy to Henry, Prince of Wales
The British Museum

70 Thomas Coryate's *Philosophical Banquet at the Mitre, Fleet Street*, 1611
PRO, S.P.14/66
Photograph

Thomas Coryate's *Crudities* includes 56 verses by friends, including Sir Rowland Cotton (33, 34) as a preface. On September 11th, 1611, Coryat invited ten of these to the Mitre to what he referred to as a 'philosophical feast' where they were 'wondrous merry'. The guests included Lionel Cranfield, later Earl of Middlesex; Sir Henry Nevill; John Donne; Sir RobertPhelps; Richard Cannock, Prince Henry's auditor; John Hoskins, lawyer and poet; Sir Henry Goodyere, the poet and emblematist; Hugo Holland; Arthur Ingram a merchant and Inigo Jones. The latter is described as:
'Nec indoctus nec profanus
Ignatius architectus'
(neither unlearned, nor uninitiated, Inigo the architect). (R.S.)

The wedding of the Princess Elizabeth and the Elector Palatine, 1613

After John de Critz (d.1642)
71 JAMES VI OF SCOTLAND AND I OF ENGLAND
Oil on panel: 57·1 × 41·9
The National Portrait Gallery (548)

74   75

Schelte Adams Bolswert (*c.*1581–1659) after Michael Jansz van Miereveldt (1567–1641)

72 ELIZABETH, ELECTRESS PALATINE, LATER QUEEN OF BOHEMIA, 1613
Engraving
The National Portrait Gallery

73 THE WEDDING PROCESSION, February 14th, 1613
Engraving from the *Beschreibung der Reiss . . .*, 1613
Photograph

Thomas Campion, *The Lords' Masque*, February 14th, 1613

74 A TORCHBEARER: A FIERY SPIRIT
Pen and ink and watercolour: 29·5 × 16 O&S 81; S&B 21
The Trustees of the Chatsworth Settlement

75 MASQUER LORD: A STAR
Pen and ink and watercolour heightened with gold and silver, now tarnished:
31·5 × 17·7 O&S 80; S&B 58
The Trustees of the Chatsworth Settlement

77

George Chapman, *The Memorable Maske*, February 15th, 1613

76 TORCHBEARER: AN INDIAN
Pen and ink and watercolour: 28·6 × 16·1 O&S 84; S&B 60
The Trustees of the Chatsworth Settlement

William Hole
77 GEORGE CHAPMAN
Engraving
Photograph

Adam Willarts (1577–1669)
78 THE ELECTOR PALATINE AND HIS BRIDE LEAVE ENGLAND, APRIL 25th, 1613
Photograph

79 FREDERICK GREETS ELIZABETH OUTSIDE HEIDELBERG, JUNE 7th, 1613
Engraving from the *Beschreibung der Reiss...*, 1613
Photograph

80 THE TOURNAMENT ON JUNE 8th, 1613: FREDERICK V AS JASON
Engraving from the *Beschreibung der Reiss...*, 1613
Photograph

Jones's work for the wedding festivities on the occasion of the marriage of James I's daughter, Elizabeth, to Frederick V, Elector Palatine, was his most ambitious to date. Following the sudden death of Prince Henry in November 1612, Jones no longer held an official position at the Jacobean court. His position was threatened too by the presence of the Prince's Italian architect, Constantino de Servi, who in fact designed in December 1613 the masque on the occasion of the marriage of Frances Howard to the Earl of Somerset. For the royal wedding, Jones designed no less than three spectac-

54

ular masques. No drawings for scenery survive, but the textual descriptions reveal an enormous advance in technical achievement. An Italian described *The Lords Masque* (74, 75) as 'very beautiful, with three changes of scene' and Campion, its author, lauds Jones's 'extraordinary industry and skill'. In it both the *scena ductilis* and the *machina versatilis* were used; there were astounding perspectives both of a wood and an architectural scene, stars (75) were made to dance and there was an obelisk of coloured lights which moved of its own volition. George Chapman, author of *The Memorable Masque*, referred to Jones as 'our kingdom's most artfull and ingenius architect Inigo Jones'. These masques must have been the climax of his stage development since 1605 and their success was recognized by the grant of the reversion of the office of the Surveyor of the King's Works on April 27th, 1613. (R.S.)

Second Italian Journey: 1613–14

Inigo was forty in 1613, and had already set out on his second climactic visit to Italy, when the reversion of the Surveyorship was officially granted on April 27th, 1613. He left England with the Earl of Arundel on the Progress to Heidelberg with the Princess Elizabeth and the Prince Palatine. They reached Heidelberg on June 7th, and spent a week there. Now the Earl's formal obligations were over and with Jones as his companion he set out via Strasbourg and Basle for an extended tour of Italy that was to last twenty-one months. Jones had not visited Italy for ten years. That first visit, which can only be located between 1597 and 1603, remains tantalizingly elusive of assessment. Then he was twenty-three; a young painter learning his craft, in Italy to 'study the arts of design'. It must be assumed that he studied the mannerist masters he loved so much: Parmigianino, Schiavone, the Carracci, and Bandinelli. Whether he collected their engravings then or later is not known, but it is certain that in 1613–14 he was instrumental in encouraging Arundel to amass his great collection of drawings by Parmigianino, and, as Mariette has pointed out, himself acquiring as many examples as possible of the work of Schiavone. Jones was now forty, the Earl was twenty-eight. Even before 1613 there was no artist in England who had absorbed so much of Italian art and theory. Jones may have deferred to the Earl's rank, but they were intimate friends, with the Earl anxious to be conducted around Italy and to build up his art collection under Jones's guidance. Arundel was the first connoisseur in England to collect in the Renaissance manner, to create cabinets out of paintings, drawings, antique sculpture, miniatures, ivories, enamels and bronzes. If Jones did not have the resources to collect in this way, he had the knowledge and there was none like him in England. As Dr A. A. Tait has written, 'both men's interest in the art of the cinquecento never faltered though their interpretations changed. To Jones, Italian art was the basis of his brilliant eclecticism: to the conservative Arundel, it was the inviolate canon of taste. From such a standpoint, the disillusioned and world-weary Earl deplored to Jones in the 1640s 'that Italy was no more Italy' and 'the Decay of Architecture, Sculpture, Painting, and all that was good and vertuous, from what not Forty Years before he had seen therein'. It Italy they reacted individually to what they saw. Jones, as an artist with a living to earn, was especially concerned with the practicalities of design, and the notes in his copy of *I Quattro Libri* reflect ideas which Arundel little understood. The Earl as a virtuoso and Junius's 'noble and cherishing mind', was interested in architecture, particularly as an intellectual experience. This may have been the rationale for the division of the drawings by Palladio and Scamozzi which they probably acquired in the Veneto, perhaps through the services of the English Ambassador, the architectural theorist Sir Henry Wotton, who owned some of Palladio's drawings. Arundel took for himself the two chests which may have contained Scamozzi's classical and didactic drawings, while he passed to Jones the workaday schemes of Palladio and Scamozzi. A similar prejudice was apparent in the contents of Arundel's architectural library. As the *Bibliotheca Norfolciana* of 1681 make clear, the formal treatise carried the day. Arundel owned three editions of Alberti's *De Re Aedificatoria*, a further three editions and a manuscript of Vitruvius, whilst he seems to have only owned Rubens's *Palazzi di Genova* of 1622, which he acquired in 1628, as a practical modern work'.

The itinerary of their travels together can be deduced from Jones's annotated Palladio, an edition of 1601 that might have been bought that year, when he was in Italy, and from the so-called Roman sketchbook which is inscribed almost arrogantly by Jones *Roma Altro diletto che Imperare non trove Inigo Jones 1614*. Lafreri's great *Speculum Romanae* was bought on this tour by Arundel, and was much delved into by Jones for whom its splendid engravings represented the twin polarities of ancient and modern Rome. The figure studies in the sketchbook, in two other albums of figure studies at Chatsworth, and in a group at Worcester College, refer extensively to his Vasari *Delle Vite de' Piu Eccelenti Pittori* of 1568, which he inscribed in Venice in 1614, and to Lomazzo's seminal *Trattate dell' Arte* of 1585 (88). We must picture Jones as travelling with at least twenty of the fifty books surviving from his library. He was the first Englishman to travel in this intellectual manner. On July 11th they entered Milan and spent about two weeks there; a week in Padua followed, then late September in Vicenza, perhaps after a visit to Venice. October in Bologna, Florence and Siena. In November they arrived in Rome, where they stayed until January 1614. In February and March they were in Naples, then back to Rome, but again in Naples on May 1st, and they were in Rome again from May 27th, at the latest, and probably through June. They saw Venice and Vicenza in August, where on the 1st they spoke with Scamozzi, but, towards the end of September they moved towards home via Genoa, Turin and Provence – where Jones drew the Pont du Gard. Christmas might have been spent in Paris, and they returned to London sometime early in January 1615. The Roman sketchbook is a redolent memorial of Jones's deep assimilation of the sixteenth-century masters. The borrowings and observations that make up his sketchbook figural style can be mirrored by the work of Guercino, whom he met, and the notes in his *Quattro Libri* (86). His own Palladian architecture reflects the influence of the aged Scamozzi, then to Jones the living embodiment of the great Palladio. In Scamozzi he must have found a marvellously sympathetic echo, for in his classicizing Palladian buildings, Scamozzi erased, as did Jones, the more mannerist tendencies of Palladio. It was momentous enough that Jones should have been able to acquire all the designs by Palladio for private and public building, but the event must have been made even more climactic if, as seems credible, Jones and Arundel were able to buy from the old and 'purblind' Scamozzi his own drawings. No single acquisition abroad has so profoundly changed the course of English architecture. Even if the old Surveyor, Simon Basil, had not conveniently died in September 1615, it is doubtful if Jones could have avoided that translation from Jacobean romantic to empirical Palladian.

(J.H.)

Part II: The British Vitruvius

Jones as a Draughtsman

The Masque Designs

Nearly five hundred designs by Inigo Jones survive for costumes and scenery for entertainments at the Stuart court from 1605 to 1640. These represent a fragment of the total which must once have existed. Even excluding his architectural designs and his little sketches of heads and drapery, his output was phenomenal especially when we realize that no drawings are known before the age of thirty-two. In 1605, in the costume designs for *The Masque of Blackness* (39, 40), Jones's draughtsmanship is within the formal Elizabethan tradition. By 1613, in the designs for Thomas Campion's *The Lords Masque* (74, 75) he is already an accomplished exponent of the free line and wash drawing. Within eight years, Jones had taught himself to draw and was the first British artist to realize the importance of this gift, which he deliberately cultivated, enabling him to realize his ideas and present them to his patrons.

The influence of Isaac Oliver (57, 58, 82) and engravings after Italian mannerist painters formed his style. Even in the sketchbook, known as the *Roman sketchbook* (89), which he took with him on his tour of Italy 1613-14, the sketches are nearly all from engraved sources. Throughout his life his technique remained practically unchanged; a sketch done in lead, brown wash and, finally, pen and brown ink. The only variation is that in the 1630s he tended to use line alone, much more than in the earlier period. His quality of draughtsmanship varied enormously, mostly according to his interest in the subject. Anti-masque costume drawings, for example, are plodding in quality whereas he never tired of doing endless sketches of the costumes for the masquers themselves.

The *Roman Sketchbook* (89) and the innumerable little sketches of heads and parts of figures derived from engraved instruction sheets of the Carracci school and from engravings after Parmigianino, Schiavone, Agostino Carracci and Bacci Bandinelli, formed his mature style. These were a constant inspiration and delight to him, as is testified by his friend Philip, 5th Earl of Pembroke in his album of mannerist engravings (The Wilton Album, The Metropolitan Museum of Art) 'Inigo Jones so fond of Parmegiano, that he bought the Prints of the Imperfect Plates, which are now here in this Book'. To these he added Giulio Parigi and Jacques Callot, whose engravings remained a quarry for his stage sets and costumes. All these artists gave him the vocabulary for his style; dramatic chiaroscuro, elongation of the figure and a sinuosity of line. His most beautiful masque drawings, although not his most original in conception, are the settings for *The Shepherd's Paradise* (301-3), *Florimène* (304-5), *Coelum Britannicum* (321-25) and *Luminalia* (333-5). Webb records Van Dyck's assessment of Jones as a draughtsman as someone 'not to be equalled by whatsoever great masters in his time for boldness, softness, sweetness, and sureness of touch'. It was a skill he failed to communicate to his pedestrian assistant, John Webb. (R.S.)

Architectural Drawings

There are no architectural drawings by Jones earlier than 1608 when he drew the projects for Britain's Burse and St Paul's Cathedral tower with Cecil's backing. These drawings are both painterly and beautiful, but apart from an advance in architectural

81   82

manners and a more delicate application of shadowing, they are still expressed in the late Elizabethan idiom of Robert Smythson. By 1615 a change has occurred, which must be due to his architectural vision of Italy on the climactic second voyage and his acquisition of the *corpus Palladianana*. Now at first hand he could see how the greatest of modern Renaissance architects drew, and this experience is reflected in the drawings of 1616 for the unknown house (192) and the Oatlands gateways. Briefly, Jones had acquired discipline, and this, combined with his new skills as a painter, render these drawings the most beautiful examples of architectural draughtsmanship in the century. For the rest of his life he has three basic manners of presentation; the painterly masque treatment with a fine pen line, delicate washes, and powerful mannerist statues for decorative sculptural embellishment. This is typified by the Newmarket Stable of 1618 (208) or the Wilton ceilings of *c*.1640 (366–69); the second manner is achieved with a lively pen, sepia ink and shadowing with cross hatching, as in the door for the Banqueting House of 1619 (213), the design for the west front of St. Paul's, *c*.1620 (247), and later in the marvellously economic doorcase for the New Cabinet Room in Somerset House in 1628 (279); thirdly, very disciplined and carefully outlined plans and elevations with a careful application of delicately shadowed washes that keep within the lines. This is the style of drawings for the Newmarket Brew House of 1618 (207) and Lord Maltravers' house of 1638 (352), both with washes, and without washes in the Arundel Lothbury elevation (354) for Lord Arundel's development at Lothbury, and for the alternative version of a house commissioned by Lord Maltravers (353). (J.H.)

John White (fl. 1585–1593)

81 A TURKISH WOMAN
Watercolours over black lead, heightened with black and white: 21·1 × 16·3
The British Museum

59

The watercolour drawings by John White of Virginian Indians and, more particularly, of exotic oriental figures, suggest the native tradition from which the early designs by Inigo Jones sprang. Both owe a great deal to the large repertory of books on costumes of the nations, of which one of the most important, Cesare Vecellio's *Habiti Antichi e moderni* (125) was used by Jones as a source book. The technique of the topographical draughtsman is the same as that used by Jones for his earliest designs for costume (126, 127). Jones quickly abandoned making such laborious costume sketches, both under the impact of a rapid development in the fluidity of his draughtsmanship and as a result of practical necessity. In order to produce all the designs for a masque production he could no longer afford the time to execute such careful studies. (R.S.)

Isaac Oliver (*c*.1566–1617)

82 DIANA

Pen and brown ink, with grey wash, over red chalk: 10·6 × 79
The British Museum

Isaac Oliver may have had a considerable influence on the rapid development of Jones's graphic style. Like Jones, he began his career working within the Elizabethan tradition, having been apprenticed to the miniaturist, Nicholas Hilliard, and he also travelled to Italy in the nineties. He was in Venice in 1596, where comparable to Jones, Parmigianino and his followers had an enormous influence on his work. Oliver was in the service of Anne of Denmark and of Henry, Prince of Wales, during the same period as Jones. Oliver's draughtsmanship was far in advance of Jones's at the outset of his career, as his drawings in the style of Parmigianino reveal. He too must have collected or had access to engravings after Italian mannerist painters. (R.S)

Italian Album

83 CASTEL SAN ANGELO
Pen, ink and wash: 23·5 × 17·5
The Trustees of the Chatsworth Settlement

84 SKETCHES AFTER LEONARDO DA VINCI
Pen, ink and wash
Chatsworth nos. 368, 369, 370
The Trustees of the Chatsworth Settlement

85 STUDY OF HEADS
Pen, ink and wash
The Trustees of the Chatsworth Settlement

The sketches have been taken out of another large Album of sketches made by Inigo Jones during his second visit to Italy. Hundreds of these drawings exist, testifying to the architect's continuous practice of the art of drawing. (R.S.)

The Sources of Jones's Mind and Imagination

See Appendix II for references

Inigo Jones . . . founded his theoretical deliberations on the metaphysical belief in the universal efficacy and beauty of numbers.[1]

What does this statement signify for architecture and how does it respond to critical examination? Jones matured as a designer entirely within the court circle, profiting from the opportunities its members gave him for foreign travel. Its every activity was a manifestation of the theory of Divine Right, a hierarchy of values emanating, as it were, from the Godhead. Referring to James I, Ben Jonson wrote:

> 'Read him as you would doe the booke
> Of all perfection and but looke
> What his proportions be;
> No measure that is thence contriv'd
> Or any motion thence deriv'd
> But is pure harmonie'[2]

Yet at the same time to place Jones intelligibly one must think of him, not in an English, but a European context.[3] What evidence is there in Europe of a philosophical outlook which might throw light on such attitudes? One of the most generative sources of Renaissance ideals in the fifteenth century was Ficino's Florentine Academy. This literary group included Alberti, scholar and architect, who defined beauty as: 'Such a Consent and Agreement of the Parts of a Whole in which it is found . . . as Congruity, that is to say, the principal law of Nature, requires.

But the Judgement which you make that a thing is beautiful does not proceed from mere opinion, but from a secret Argument and Discourse in the Mind itself.'[4]

A truly Platonic approach, reflecting an attitude of great antiquity. Its origins lie with Pythagoras, who related linear dimensions to musical pitch (the harmonic ratios), and with Plato's cosmology. Plato, drawing on Pythagorean sources, developed a mathematical structuring of the universe according to a comprehensive system of harmonic ratios involving the three mean proportionals.[5] This theme was developed in the third century A.D. by Plotinus of Alexandria, relating it to Eastern religious traditions. Central to Plotinus' imagery lies the permeation of the Light of the Godhead through to the physical world; qualitatively by personal absorption into the mystical unity of creation (man as microcosm of the universe); quantitatively by the Pythagorean/Platonic number system.[6] The twin themes of *Light* and *Measure*.[7] This philosophical system, known as Neo-platonism, was absorbed by Augustine and thus by Western Christianity.[8] All these influences culminated in the twelfth century School of Chartres. Later, having assimilated the onslaught of Thomistic Aristotelianism, they were revitalized through the comprehensive activities of the fifteenth-century Florentine Academy, by the Pléiade in France a century later, and, in an obscure form, by Raleigh's School of Night, which included Marlowe and Chapman. Amongst the numerous architectural treatises of the period, based on the writing of Vitruvius, the themes of *Light* and *Measure* were immanent in those of Alberti, Palladio and Barbaro's commentaries on Vitruvius. These three seminal works were closely analysed by Jones.

Let us now try to approach the sources of Jones's thinking from three angles. Firstly his background, that is, his patrons and his circle; secondly, his struggle to attain parity of status for the architect with the court intellectuals; and finally his work, comprising the masque designs, his writing, and his buildings. Jones's patrons, whether members of the Royal family or prominent courtiers,[9] had all travelled abroad and many of them were well acquainted with intellectual opinion in Italy and France. With Arundel, a well-informed connoisseur and patron of the arts, Jones made one of his Italian journeys, during which he studied assiduously. Among his professional associates, Salomon de Caus and Henry Peacham are known to have written works based on Neo-platonic theory.[10] Not only was he a friend of Chapman, but he associated with Donne at the Mermaid Tavern. He probably knew John Dowland and Sir Henry Wotton. All four men were familiar with these principles.

Inigo's collaboration as masque designer with Ben Jonson is well known. Their subsequent quarrel, however, apart from personal jealousy, concerned a professional issue. The architect was anxious to achieve parity with the poets who still dominated the cultural scene. Fascinating evidence of this is suggested by the proscenium of a masque designed by Jones shortly after Jonson's dismissal, *Albion's Triumph*. It contained two allegorical figures entitled *Theorica* and *Practica*, derived from Scamozzi. The distinction between these two aspects of design follows the direct tradition of Alberti, Barbaro, Palladio and others. The argument is advanced that the mental act of conceiving the idea is independent of that of giving visual form to it. It was through such Platonic arguments that European architects had been striving to bring architecture to the status of a liberal art for a hundred and fifty years.[11] Even further to rid themselves of the slur of being mere craftsmen, they had founded, with the painters and sculptors, a number of Academies of Design, where these themes were debated.[12]

There is collateral evidence from Jonson's satirical anti-masques that Inigo was preoccupied with harmonic ratios. In one of these, a character burlesquing the architect is speaking:

'Well done, my Musicall, Arithmeticall, Geometricall gamsters! . . . It is carried in number, weight and measure, as if the Airs were all Harmonie and the Figures a well-timed Proportion.'[13]

Indeed, Jonson's literary contributions to the masques were themselves redolent with Platonic overtones. This is not surprising, for the Royal Masques, a confluence of all the arts, were subject to the censorship of the Lord Chamberlain, and were intended not only to give pleasure to a sophisticated audience, but were also an instrument of state policy:

'by all means to reduce tempestuous and turbulent natures into a sweet calm of civil concord'.[14]

Inigo's writings are almost entirely confined to the marginal comments in his books, but these are extensive and revealing. Critical examination of the marginalia in the three architectural treatises already cited leads us to discern certain attitudes characteristic of Neo-platonic thinking.[15] A few examples may serve to give the flavour of the comments. Against one passage of Barbaro's philosophical discourse he paraphrased the core of the argument:

'Eurythmia or fayr number is gratous aspects in composition of the members,' and, later, 'Eurithmia is the temperinge of the proportion applied to ye matter as Equiti is to justice.'[16] Many references to the musical analogy (the harmonic proportions) accompany the relevant passages in Alberti, as, for instance:

'the same numbers that please the eare pleese the eie.'[17] Against the anthropomorphic analogy in the Vitruvian text (Plotinus' man as microcosm of the universe) he writes:

'the boddi of man well proporsioned is the patern for proportion in buildings'.[18] But Inigo was no pendant. A spontaneous comment in his Palladio runs:
'but alwaes the libberty of composing w^t reason is not taken away but who followes ye best of ye ancients cannot much earr'.[19]

What, finally, is the evidence from his buildings? Sir John Summerson has drawn attention to the small number of architectural elements which Jones chose to combine and recombine.[20] This in itself suggests a preoccupation with significant relationships while analysis of the designs of the major works demonstrates conclusively the immanence of the harmonic proportions. The following are the principal ratios. These are all encountered in graphic analysis, some of them frequently.[21]

$$1.1. \qquad 1.2 \qquad 2.3 \qquad 3.4$$
$$1.2.4 \qquad 4.6.9 \qquad 9.12.16$$
$$1.2.3 \qquad \begin{cases} 3.6.8 \\ 3.4.8 \end{cases} \qquad 8.9$$

It is evident that Inigo Jones, as did so many of the great Renaissance artists on the mainland of Europe, viewed architecture and, indeed, the other arts, as an opportunity, if not an obligation, to echo the structuring of the universe as it was then understood; to reawaken man to the reality of deeper truth than lies in the world of appearances.

Just as the work of Newton, drawing on that of Kepler, was soon seriously to disturb the traditional basis of Platonic cosmology, the Civil War shook Jones's world to its foundations. The Revolution of 1688 liquidated it. The Whig oligarchy, permeated by the Empirical philosophy of Locke, created the architectural School of Burlington. How far did they and their successors comprehend Jones's mind?

After all, Horace Walpole, writing within ten years of Burlington's death, said that the Banqueting House stood as 'a model of the most pure and beautiful taste'.[22] A more misleading summary of Jones' methods and capabilities can hardly be conceived.

Gordon Toplis

Inigo Jones's Library
See Appendix II

Some forty-five of Jones's books are preserved at Worcester College, the gift of Dr George Clarke in 1736. The actual date of their purchase from descendants of John Webb is not known, but Clarke owned Jones's drawings by *c.*1703. A few other books from Jones's library are elsewhere, notably Barbaro's edition of *Vitruvius* of 1567 at Chatsworth (87) and Lomazzo's *Trattato* in the Sabin collection (88). His copy of Serlio's *Tutti L'Opere d'Architettura et Prospettiva*, published in 1569, is in the library at The Queen's College, Oxford (92). Also, Dr Clarke made an accurate copy of the extensive annotations in his own Serlio of the same date, and that is now among his own books in Worcester College. What proportion of Jones's library these represent is impossible to determine, but by the standards of the age it is a large and valuable collection. If we can judge Jones's tastes by it, they were serious and professional; nothing so frivolous as literature is included. Jones was not a classical scholar. He obtained his knowledge of classical antiquity and its culture secondhand, through Italian translations of standard authors and through works by humanist popularizers who synthesized within the terms of their own philosophy the Greek and Roman past as it was viewed by the Renaissance. Therefore Plato is represented by *The Republic*, Aristotle by the *Ethics*, and Plutarch by the *Morals*, all in Italian translations. History is for the most part ancient, and again in Italian, including the works of Herodotus, Dio Cassius and Caesar, the last in translation by Palladio.

The largest part of the library is, of course, concerned with architecture, and Jones's admiration for Palladio is amply witnessed by the detailed annotations in his splendid copy of the *Architettura* in a 1601 edition (86). However, an understanding of Jones's philosophical attitude, as a Neo-platonist towards architecture, is better gained by a reading of the ample annotations in the Vitruvius, the Alberti, and the Lomazzo. Not surprisingly, one of the most fully annotated books is the Serlio, but there is evidence that Jones read his books by Cataneo, Philbert de L'Orme, Rusconi and Scamozzi thoroughly. Of related interest are the few works on Roman antiquity and war machinery. Some of these were illustrated with pictures of the monuments of antiquity from which he borrowed freely both for his architecture and his stage sets; also included are early engineering devices (e.g. pulleys, levers etc) which must have contributed to the development of his stage machinery. In particular it is interesting to know that one of his painters, Mathew Goodericke, owned in 1621 Domenico Fontana's *Della Transportatione Dell'Obelisco Vaticano* (now in Mr and Mrs Paul Mellon's collection), a key source for pulleys and balancing devices. Jones's extensive scribblings in Lorini's *Fortificationi* shows that he read this book more thoroughly than any other, and it is a reminder that he belongs to a long-established Renaissance tradition for whom military engineering was a *sine qua non* of any architect's studies. This presumably bore fruit in the Civil War, when Jones's expertise in fortification must have been of considerable value to the King's defences, and it was probably for this purpose that he was at the siege of Basing House in 1645, alas to no avail. There is one volume of Vasari's *Vite* bearing a notation that he had it with him in Venice in 1614; the marginalia indicate that he was most interested in the lives of the architects Fra Giocondo and Antonio Sangallo. Strabo's *Geografia*, in Italian, originally belonged to Scamozzi, and seems to have annotations in his hand as well as in Jones's. The only work bearing directly on the Court masque is Vincenzo Cartari's *Le imagini de i dei de gli antichi*, 1592, a standard iconographic handbook addressed primarily to students, which dealt with the whole pantheon of the classical gods, glossing their persons and their lives with a moral meaning which formed the basis for their appearance in the masques. Surprisingly, there is neither a Valeriano nor a Ripa (93) nor the texts of any of the several Italian court productions, which Jones directly adapted. Perhaps, less surprisingly, there is nothing by the masque authors Jonson, Campion, Daniel, Carew, Townshend, Shirley or Davenant. The only work in English is Arthur Hopton's *Topographical Glasse* of 1611. (J.H. S.O. R.S.)

86 Andrea Palladio, *I Quattro Libri dell'Architettura*, Venice 1601
The Provost and Fellows of Worcester College

Part of Dr George Clarke's bequest, this copy of Palladio has not always remained with Inigo Jones's library. Clarke bought it on March 3rd, 1709 from the engraver Michael Burghers, who probably acquired it, when he dated it, April 21st, 1694. He had also owned the Queen's College Serlio. It may have been detached from Jones's library after Webb's death in 1672, but this is not absolutely certain. The volume was extensively annotated by Jones after 1613, when he presumably bought it in Italy. A date in the volume *1601 dei docato Ven* has often been quoted as proof that it was bought in Venice in 1601. This is most unlikely and refers instead to the fact that the book is the Venice 1601 edition. Had Jones bought it then there would surely have occurred entries dated between 1601 and 1613, whereas there are none. This book is perhaps one of the most famous of any annotated by an Englishman, for the results of Jones's reading, translations and comments were to have a traumatic effect upon English architecture, and subsequently upon the dissemination of Palladianism. This should not blind us to the fact that there are many other annotated volumes in Jones's library which provide an equally startling insight into his reading of Renaissance theorists. Notable are Daniele Barbaro's edition of Vitruvius (87); Scamozzi's *Idea della Architettura Universale*, Venice, 1615, which Jones bought on March 25th, 1617; Bartoli's *L'Architettura di Leon Batista Alberti*, Monreale 1565; and Lorini's *Fortificationi* 1609, which is amply annotated by him. This copy of Palladio's *Architettura* is of seminal importance, if only intrinsically and symbolically. On one page Jones writes, paraphrasing Palladio, 'to varry is good but not to part from ye Preceptes of the arrte'. Such precepts are not to be found here, for these we must turn to Vitruvius and Alberti. However, more than any other book, Jones seems to have jotted comments into it throughout his life. The terminal leaves are redolent of his advancing old age, with disclosures that 'Copulation must be utterly escheued for that thereby the best blud of a man is wasted', or 'Item to break wind uppwarded when you cast in the mornings doth lossen mellencoly and causeth it to pass downwardes the better'. (J.H.)

87 MARCUS VITRUVIUS POLLIO, *De Architectura Libri Decem*, Venice 1567
Inigo Jones's annotated copy
The Trustees of the Chatsworth Settlement

The only complete treatise on architecture to survive from antiquity (Vitruvius was an obscure Roman architect active 46–30 B.C.), it was first printed *c.*1486. There were many editions, the most famous being the Como 1521 edition with commentary by Cesare Cesariano. The most learned intellectually, however, was this one of 1567 edited by Daniele Barbaro for whom Palladio not only drew the plates, but designed Barbaro's superb villa at Maser. Basically the Vitruvian text is obscure and was therefore widely interpreted by Renaissance architects from Alberti onwards. Jones's notes show that he and Palladio had the same understanding, namely that the Vitruvian text must be used with caution and determined by a study of the buildings themselves. This conforms to the Lomazzian precept that it is best to travel and see the finest artists' work and only then to draw up rules of study. As in the *Roman Sketchbook* (89), Jones writes in his Vitruvius *altro diletto che imparar non trevo*. On Book IV, page 163 Jones refers to his design for an architrave at Somerset House in relation to an Arundel marble with gorgon's heads. This marble was recently excavated on the site of Arundel House and is the same as that depicted by Van Dyck in the *Continence of Scipio*, painted for the Duke of Buckingham about 1621. The marble was therefore once in Buckingham's collection, but had quite clearly passed to Arundel by the time Jones designed his architrave at Somerset House. This was part of the Chapel closet designed *c.*1630, where, as in the antique marble, the frieze is decorated with volutes between the gorgon's heads rather than triglyphs as in a correct Doric frieze. In the Ashmolean Museum is a drawing of this marble seen by John Webb in 1639. (J.H.)

88 G. P. Lomazzo, *Trattato dell'Arte della Pittura, Scultura et Architettura*, Milan 1584
Inigo Jones's annotated copy
Collection of Mr Sidney Sabin, London

89

89 ROMAN SKETCHBOOK Opened out with Jones's translation and drawings, illustrative 'of the propotion of children' from Lomazzo *Trattato*, Book 6, folio 290.
The Trustees of the Chatsworth Settlement

90 Lomazzo, *Trattato dell'Arte della Pittura, Scultura et Architettura*, Milan 1584
Book 6, folio 290 with annotations
Photograph

The appeal of Lomazzo to Jones must have been tremendous. It was the only theoretical treatise to be translated in part into English by Richard Haydock in 1598. As a book, the Lomazzo is to Jones the painter what the Palladio is to Jones the architect. Lomazzo formed one of the group of academic Milanese mannerists, one of twin polarities, the other being the Academy of Drawing in Rome whose dominant member was Federico Zuccaro. Jones digested the precepts of Lomazzo eagerly, especially those concerned with Neo-platonic theory, the nature of beauty, anti-rationalism and his recommendations for the training of artists, which stated fundamentally that art can be taught by precept. Rules of study can be established by looking at the work of all the best artists. This is the method established by Lomazzo in his *Idea del Tempio della Pittura* of 1590, a book Jones must have possessed. (J.H.)

91 Sebastiano Serlio, *Tutte l'Opera d'Architettura, et Prospetiva*, Venice 1619
Royal Institute of British Architects Library

This was John Webb's annotated copy, and a subsequent owner, Sir James Thornhill signed the title page and wrote *This was Inigo Jones Book/ afterwards Mr Webbs/ then Mr Churchills/ then Sr J Thornhills*, but as far as the annotations are concerned, they are entirely in Webb's hand. Jones used Serlio long before 1619, and as a pattern book Jones regarded Serlio as an inexhaustible quarry from as early as 1606 for the masques (an unknown entertainment) and in 1608 for architecture (Cecil's projects, 28–32). In Jones's work, there is always discriminating refinement in contrast to the often literal and crude transpositions by the late Elizabethan architects and his contemporaries. Jones's way of looking at Serlio is no better illustrated than in his marvellous series of designs for gateways (387–89). (J.H.)

92 Sebastiano Serlio, *Tutti l'Opera d'Architettura, et Prospetiva*, Venice *c*.1560–62
The Provost and Fellows of The Queen's College

This was Inigo Jones's annotated copy of Serlio, from which Dr George Clarke accurately transcribed the architect's notes. Clarke's copy is among his own books, which he bequeathed along with Inigo Jones's library to Worcester College in 1736. (J.H.)

Jones as a Connoisseur

Inigo Jones collected both architectural drawings by Palladio and Scamozzi and engravings, particularly by mannerist artists. These he used as a quarry for ideas, but Jones was also regarded in his time as a connoisseur. He is described in 1636, attended by the King, looking through a consignment of old master paintings which had just arrived. He 'threw off his coat, put on his eye glasses, took a candle and, together with the King, began to examine them very closely'. Prince Henry, for whom Jones had built a gallery at St James's, was the first person deliberately to build up a collection of Italian Renaissance pictures and bronzes and of classical antiquities. Whether Jones was a formative influence or not on that collection is unknown, but from 1616 onwards he was certainly closely connected with Arundel's purchases of works of art. In April 1616 Arundel ordered a consignment of paintings to be delivered in his absence to Jones who was clearly acting as a receiving agent, advising Arundel which to choose for his collection.

Van der Dort's catalogue of Charles I's collection is peppered with references to items purchased or presented by Mr Surveyor. These include a tapestry cartoon of Diana and Callisto, a drawing of Prince Henry at the barriers, a wax portrait of Henry VIII, a perspective of a prison, and a 'Book in folio of Annatame done after Phasario' (Vasari?). Jones was also commissioned in 1632 to catalogue the King's collection of antique coins. His connexion with these seminal collections, those formed by Prince Henry, Arundel and Charles I, is suggestive that he must have been a powerful driving force behind the idea of the collection which in itself was a new one in England. Elizabethan houses had contained portraits almost exclusively and those hung in the Long Gallery. The Renaissance concept of the cabinet with its paintings, exquisite bronzes, miniatures, classical antiquities and rare curiosities reflected both the idea of the gentleman as the *virtuoso* (propogated by Henry Peacham in his handbooks) and as the *maecenas*, whose status in society was enhanced by the possession of such treasures. This new apparatus of nobility was systematically promoted by Arundel, Pembroke, Somerset and Buckingham. The impact of the paintings, especially of the Venetian School which they imported, is well-known, but a study of the influence of the collections of classical antiquities might be even more revealing in explaining the revolution in taste and visual style achieved by Jones. (R.S.)

Sources for Jones's Masque Designs

Books

93 CESARE RIPA, *Iconologia*, 1593, Padua, 1611 (1610)
The British Museum

The most famous and influential encyclopedia of classical iconography was the *Iconologia* of Cesare Ripa (*c*.1560–*c*.1625), first published at Rome in 1593, and frequently reissued in expanded versions until late in the eighteenth century. Based not only on earlier mythographers, but also on such visual sources as coins and medals, ·*Iconologia* became a standard handbook both for the imagery of the ancient gods and for their translation into moral and philosophical concepts as well. In *Iconologia*, the rationalizing tendencies of Renaissance thinking have full play, and mythology is seen as a way of conceptualizing abstractions; Olympian deities become nothing more than the embodiments of natural forces, or externalisations of the inner qualities of men. Essentially analytic and philosophical, less exclusively directed toward painters and sculptors than other iconographies of the period, Ripa's was the ideal source book for the creator of masques, with their complex philosophical allegories, and both Jones and his collaborators relied heavily on it. (S.O.)

94 BELLEROPHON AND THE CHIMAERA, *c*.1610
Pen and black ink washed with greenish brown: 20·8 × 17·1 O&S 33; S&B 416
The Trustees of the Chatsworth Settlement

95 VIRTÙ
Wood engraving from Cesare Ripa, *Iconologia*, Padua, 1610
Photograph

96 GIOVANNI PIERIO VALERIANO BOLZANA, *Hieroglyphica*, 1602
The British Museum

As Ripa's was the handbook of iconology, Giovanni Pierio Valeriano (1477–1558) complied the standard encyclopedia of symbolism, the *Hieroglyphica*, first published at Basel in 1556, and frequently reprinted. Originally conceived as a manual of Egyptian and Neo-platonic hieroglyphs, and addressed to an elite circle of scholars and philosophers, the book in its published form is a remarkably wide-ranging lexicon of visual meaning, key to a way of thinking and mode of expression that reached its highest flowering in the Renaissance. If Ripa provided the figures for a Renaissance allegory, Valeriano provided its visual language, and both works supplied Jones and his poets with a crucial link between the arts of the present and the wisdom of the past. (S.O.)

Engravings

Throughout his working career Jones was a relentless plagiarist, a magpie artist who lifted from a multiplicity of sources ideas for scenery and costumes. Jones himself must have had a very substantial collection of engravings which he used as a working quarry, an encyclopaedia of images to which he had constant recourse. Sometimes, as in the Roman Amphitheatre for *Albion's Triumph* (102) he lifts the design for his back

94

95

99

100

101

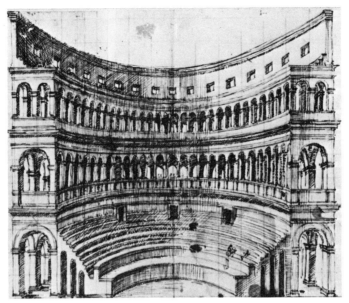

102

shutter line for line from its engraved source (103); on other occasions, as in the winter *intermedium* in *Floriméne* (111) he takes a section from an engraving, disregarding elements of the composition not required for his stage picture. (R.S.)

97 HERCULES' BOWL BEARER in *Pleasure Reconciled to Virtue*, 1618
Pen and black ink: 18·5 × 25·5 O&S 92; S&B 46
The Trustees of the Chatsworth Settlement

Marcantonio Raimondi (b.*c*.1480, d.1527/34)
98 ANTIQUE SARCOPHAGUS
Engraving
Photograph

99 A STREET IN PERSPECTIVE in *The Vision of Delight*, 1617
O&S 89; S&B 370
Photograph

100 THE TRAGIC SCENE
Wood engraving from Sebastiano Serlio, *Tutte L'Opere d'Architettura et Prospettiva*
Photograph

101 THE COMIC SCENE
Wood engraving from Sebastiano Serlio, *Tutte L'Opere d'Architettura et Prospettiva*
Photograph

102 AN AMPHITHEATRE in '*Albion's Triumph*', 1632
Pen and brown ink squared with black lead for enlargement, and splashed with brown scene-painters' distemper: 28·3 × 32·6 O&S 192; S&B 121
The Trustees of the Chatsworth Settlement

71

103

103 ROMAN AMPHITHEATRE
Engraving from Onuphrius Panvinus, *De Ludis Circensibus*, 1581
Photograph

Anti-masquers in '*Albion's Triumph*', 1632

104 SALTATOR OR TUMBLERS
Pen and brown ink washed with grey: 17·4×98 O&S 194; S&B 113
The Trustees of the Chatsworth Settlement

105 PUGILI OR BUFFETERS
Pen and brown ink washed with grey: 16·5×9·7 O&S 195; S&B 114
The Trustees of the Chatsworth Settlement

106 SATYRS LIKE DANCERS
Pen and brown ink washed with grey: 16·3×8·6 O&S 196; S&B 115
The Trustees of the Chatsworth Settlement

107 CYTHROEDUS
Pen and brown ink washed with grey: 16·3×10·2 O&S 202; S&B 130
The Trustees of the Chatsworth Settlement

108 ROMAN IMPERIAL TRIUMPH
Engraving from Onuphrius Panvinus, *De Ludis Circensibus*, 1581
Photograph

111

109 A GARDEN AND A PRINCELY VILLA in '*Coelum Britannicum*', 1634
O&S 281 ; S&B 247
Photograph

Antonio Tempesta (1555–1630)
110 A GARDEN
Engraving
Photograph

111 THE INTERMEDIUM OF WINTER in *Florimène*, 1635
Pen and brown ink, squared with black lead for enlargement: 22·6 × 31·5
O&S 329; S&B 246
The Trustees of the Chatsworth Settlement

73

112

Antonio Tempesta (1555–1630)

112 WINTER
Engraving
Photograph

113 NIGHT in *Luminalia*, 1638
Pen and brown ink washed with dark grey, splashed with blue scene-painters'
distemper: 16·2 × 22·1 O&S 384; S&B 309
The Trustees of the Chatsworth Settlement

Hendrik Goudt (1585–*c*.1630) after Adam Elsheimer (1574–1620)

114 THE FLIGHT INTO EGYPT
Engraving
Photograph

Jacques Callot (*c*.1592–1635)

Jones first drew on the engravings of Callot in 1631 for his series of anti-masque designs
for *Love's Triumph through Callipolis* (118). The *commedia dell'arte* figures of the *Balli di
Sfessania* with their bizarre costumes and sinuous dancing movement were a major
source of inspiration to Jones in the creation of anti-masques throughout the 1630's.
Occasionally he drew on other engravings by Callot for scenery as in the case of the
back shutter of a garden which is a contracted version of *Le Grand Parterre de Nancy*
(123). The Furies in the last of the masques, *Salmacida Spolia*, are based partly on the
snake-haired hags that precede a chariot at the *Barriers* of 1627 at Nancy (125). Callot's
late mannerist twisting sinuosity of line, together with his theatrical use of *chiaroscuro*

Dutch Post

115

Operator.

116

effects to achieve distance, had a direct appeal to Jones. In this way, Callot had a great influence on the formation of Jones's graphic style in the 1630's. (R.S.)

115 A DWARF POST FROM HELL in *Chlorida*, 1631
Pen and brown ink washed with grey: 16·5 × 13·4 O&S 170; S&B 87
The Trustees of the Chatsworth Settlement

116 WOLFGANGUS VANDERGOOSE in *Salmacida Spolia*, 1640
Pen and black ink washed with grey; 18·2 × 11·4 O&S 419; S&B 331
The Trustees of the Chatsworth Settlement

Jacques Callot (*c*.1592–1635)
117 DWARF in *Varie Figure Gobbi*
Engraving
Photograph

118 AN ANGRY QUARRELLING LOVER in *Love's Triumph through Callipolis*, 1631
Pen and brown ink washed with grey: 18·7 × 11·3 O&S 157; S&B 76
The Trustees of the Chatsworth Settlement

75

122

Jacques Callot (*c.*1592–1635)

119 SPANISH CAPTAIN
Engraving
Photograph

120 A WHINING BALLADING LOVER in *Love's Triumph through Callipolis*, 1631
Pen and brown ink washed with grey: 17·1 × 9·8 O&S 150; S&B 169
The Trustees of the Chatsworth Settlement

Jacques Callot (*c.*1592–1635)

121 TITLEPAGE of the *Balli di Sfessania*
Engraving
Photograph

122 A GARDEN: BACK SHUTTER, probably for *The Shepherd's Paradise*, 1631
Pen and brown ink, squared up, torn and damaged: 28·1 × 33·2 O&S 252; S&B 208
The Trustees of the Chatsworth Settlement

76

123

Jacques Callot (*c.*1592–1635)
123 LE GRAND PARTERRE DE NANCY, 1625
Engraving
Photograph

124 FURIES in *Salmacida Spolia*, 1640
Photograph: O&S 416; S&B 324
The Trustees of the Chatsworth Settlement

Jacques Callot (*c.*1592–1635)
125 'L'ENTRÉE DE MONSIEUR DE COUVANGE ET DE MONSIEUR DE CHALABRE' in the *Combat à la Barrière*, 1627
Engraving
Photograph

Vecellio, 'Habiti Antichi...'

Throughout his career Inigo Jones made use of Cesare Vecellio's celebrated costume book, of which he apparently possessed the 1598 edition. This we can deduce from the fact that Jones uses certain illustrations that first appear in that edition. Vecellio is drawn on for the creation of the earliest of his masquing dresses, those for Anne of Denmark and her ladies as Ethiopian Virgins in *The Masque of Blackness* (39, 40). Here Jones combined the looped mantle and striped skirt, which appear in an illustration of a young Ethiopian girl, with a cut-away skirt derived from the dress of an Ethiopian soldier and a bead-dress based on that of a Thessalonian bride. The use of Vecellio spans Jones's working career, sometimes quarried in overt form as in the Polish Knight (127, 128) or for the captives in *Albion's Triumph* (129, 130), sometimes used as a

77

127   128

source of inspiration and adapted as in Jones's numerous feathered Indian costumes, from the Torchbearers in Chapman's *The Memorable Masque* (76) to Indamora in *The Temple of Love*. (R.S.)

126 CESARE VECELLIO, *Habiti antichi et moderni di tutto il mondo . . .*, Venice, 1598
The British Museum

127 POLISH KNIGHT, before 1613
Pen and brown ink washed with brown: 29·7 × 18 O&S 42; S&B 9
The Trustees of the Chatsworth Settlement

128 POLISH HABIT
Wood engraving from Cesare Vecellio, *Habiti antichi et moderni di tutto il mondo . . .*, Venice, 1598
Photograph

129 CAPTIVE in *Albion's Triumph*, 1632
Pen and brown ink washed with grey: 15 × 9·6 O&S 212; S&B 138
The Trustees of the Chatsworth Settlement

130 YOUNG WOMAN OF ALEPPO
Wood engraving from Cesare Vecellio, *Habiti antichi et moderni di tutto il mondo . . .*, Venice, 1598
Photograph

135

The Florentine 'Intermezzi'

Practically every setting for the masques covering the period 1631 to 1640, from *Love's Triumph through Callipolis* to *Salmacida Spolia*, was directly lifted from engravings of scenery created by the Parigi for the Florentine *intermezzi*. It is curious to compare Jones's increasing fluency of draughtsmanship with his declining originality of vision. The dependence on Florentine sources, however, has misled historians of the development of stage mechanics, to assume that Jones also used the same system of machines and scenic change. This does not necessarily follow, and it is doubtful whether Jones ever saw a Florentine production on stage. The plagiarism does not lessen either the emblematic power of the stage pictures to Whitehall audiences, to which the Palace of Fame in *Britannia Triumphans* (137) or the Storm in *Salmacida Spolia* (139), in spite of their sources, had quite different meanings from what they originally had for the court of the Tuscan Grand Dukes. (R.S.)

131 THE VALE OF TEMPE in *Tempe Restored*
O&S 216; S&B 139
Photograph

Giulio Parigi (d.1635)
132 THE GARDEN OF CALYPSO in *Il Giudizio di Paride*, 1608
Engraving
Photograph

133 AN INDIAN SHORE in *The Temple of Love*, 1635
O&S 295; S&B 229
Photograph

79

136

Remigio Cantagallina, 1582–1630, after Giulio Parigi, d.1635

134 THE FLEET OF AMERIGO VESPUCCI in *Il Giudizio di Paride*, 1608
Engraving
Photograph

135 A HORRID HELL in *Britannia Triumphans*, 1638
O&S 336; S&B 193
Photograph

Alfonso Parigi (d.1656)

136 THE REALM OF PLUTO in *La Flora*, 1628
Engraving
Photograph

137 THE PALACE OF FAME in *Britannia Triumphans*, 1638
Pen and brown ink over incised lines: 32·5 × 24·1 O&S 340; S&B 299
The Trustees of the Chatsworth Settlement

Remigio Cantagallina, 1582–1630, after Giulio Parigi, d.1635

138 THE PALACE OF FAME in *Il Giudizio di Paride*, 1608
Engraving
Photograph

139 A STORM AND A TEMPEST in *Salmacida Spolia*, 1640
O&S 410; S&B 323
Photograph

Alfonso Parigi (d.1656)

140 STORM SCENE in *La Flora*, 1628
Engraving
Photograph

139

140

Jones and Stonehenge

In 1620 King James commissioned Jones to investigate the mysterious monoliths of Stonehenge. The results of this study, published only posthumously by John Webb, constitute one of the most remarkable pieces of evidence we possess about the way Jones's imagination worked. He begins by rejecting the traditional association of the structure with Druids, a pastoral people with no architecture to speak of; both the proportions of the building and the mechanical sophistication necessary to move and erect its huge stones lead him to believe that its origin is Roman. A variety of evidence is adduced to support this view: the monoliths are of the Tuscan order, the most austere and ancient of the Roman architectural orders; a plan similar to that of Stonehenge is to be found in Vitruvius; the circles and triangles basic to its scheme had mystical significance for classical theology. The only part of this reasoning that is accurate is the rejection of the Druids; the rest is at times illogical, at times pure fantasy, but always profoundly informed by Jones's vision of Britain as the true heir of Roman culture. The architect devises a severe and elegant reconstruction of the building as a Roman temple, open to the heavens, and dedicated to Coelus, or Uranus, the oldest of the gods in the classical pantheon. The purest and noblest example of Roman religious architecture is thus established in Britain.

Jones's thesis about Stonehenge constitutes a striking assertion of Renaissance faith. To the Ancients Coelus was in fact not a god, but merely a personification of the heavens; he was never worshiped and no temple was ever dedicated to him. But Renaissance writers who saw Christianity as a fulfillment of classical culture viewed the mythological Coelus as an imperfectly realized version of God the Father. Jones in dedicating Stonehenge to Coelus is in fact not classicising it but Christianising it, and, moreover, in a very Protestant way as well. Catholic churches bear the names of particular figures in a large and various pantheon, but the architect does not see in Stonehenge a temple of Mercury or Apollo or Diana. What he sees is the church reformed and purified, a structure consecrated solely to the worship of God the Father. (s.o.)

141 John Webb, after Inigo Jones, *The Most Notable Antiquity of Great Britain called Stone-Heng, Restored,* 1655
Collection of Mr John Harris

142 John Webb, *A Vindication of Stone-Heng, Restored,* 1665
Collection of Mr John Harris

Stone-heng Restored, published by Jones's executor three years after his death, was based on notes made by the architect during the course of a study of the monument commissioned by King James. The work purports to be autobiographical, and is one of our few sources of information about Jones's early life; it contains brief accounts of a youthful trip to Italy, and the growth of an intense interest in classical architecture while there. Though much of Jones's thesis is untenable, the basic observations are sound, and the conclusion – that Stonehenge was a temple consecrated not to a particular deity in the Roman pantheon, but to Coelus, the god of Heaven – has been startlingly vindicated by recent scholars, who have determined the monument to have

141

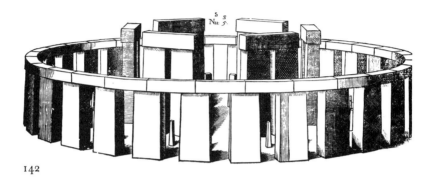

142

been designed as an astronomical observatory. The essay was taken very seriously in its own time, and became the centre of a controversy that lasted well into the next century. It is illustrated, unfortunately, only with crude woodcuts, presumably based on drawings by Jones, though in the elaborate third edition of 1725 these were replaced with very elegant engravings. (s.o.)

The Mechanical Development of Jones's Stage

In order to achieve his miraculous scenic effects Jones required to be an expert in engineering. In the introduction to Book X of Vitruvius, which is on motion and machines, the author states that it is a branch of the architects's sphere of activity to plan seating and machinery for public shows and plays on the stage. Book X of Vitruvius discusses machinery of all kinds, both military and peaceful; pulleys, wheels, pumps, screws, water organs, engines for military defence and attack; as well as amusing toys worked by pneumatic devices and devices for theatrical shows. From this stemmed the role of the Renaissance architect as a scenic engineer. It is a tradition Jones may have been familiar with early in life through translations of these sections of Vitruvius by John Dee in his *Preface to Euclid*, 1570.

It is clear that although Jones may at some stage have had access abroad to a 'picture frame stage' of the type evolved for the *intermezzi* of 1589 (134, 136, 138, 140)

83

his stage mechanics were largely self-invented. We can trace his development over the years as he achieves ever more spectacular effects. Central to his masque visions throughout was an upper and lower stage, on the former of which he placed celestial visions to be revealed from time to time. Proscenium arches in the main stayed square until he invented the fly gallery in *Chloridia*, when the curtain arose for the first time and Fame, at the close, slowly ascended. Machines too were gradually perfected. In 1606 clouds bearing masquers gently sloped down for the first time, instead of descending like a bucket into a well, as one observer wrote, and by the early thirties Jones could lower five deities from the fly gallery in a cloud to stage level, whisking the cloud away, to reveal them in a golden throne. In *Luminalia*, in 1638, he closed with his most ambitious heavenly spectacle, an aerial ballet. All this reveals a mastery of mechanics, but very few designs and drawings survive to reveal how these effects were actually achieved. The most important ones from the point of construction and machinery are gathered here to illustrate how he developed the stage as a machine. (R.S.)

Plans, Elevations, Diagrams and Models

143 DIAGRAM OF THE SET for Ben Jonson's *Love Freed from Ignorance and Folly*, 1611
Photograph
The diagram shows the stage at the moment when the Queen and ladies, the Daughters of the Morn, are released from their prison. Clouds concealing the upper stage have parted; the ladies sit on three turning machines, which revolve, allowing them to descend and enter through the central gateway. Structurally this bipartite design, with the upper section used not as a playing area but as a compound machine, represents the basic form of Jones's stage. (S.O.)

Inigo Jones, *Florimène*, 1635

144 PLAN OF THE STAGE AND AUDITORIUM
B. M. Landsdowne MS 1171, fol.5–6   O&S 321 ; S&B 240
Photograph

145 GROUND PLAN OF THE STAGE
B. M. Lansdowne MS 1171, fol.15–16   O&S 322 ; S&B 241
Photograph

146 DIAGRAM OF GROUND PLAN OF THE STAGE
O&S fig.103
Photograph

147 ELEVATION OF THE STAGE
B. M. Lansdowne MS 1171, fol.7–8   O&S 323
Photograph

148 DIAGRAM OF ELEVATION OF THE STAGE
O&S fig.104
Photograph

149 SECTION OF THE STAGE AND SCENERY
B. M. Lansdowne MS 1171 fol.13–14   O&S 324 ; S&B 242
Photograph

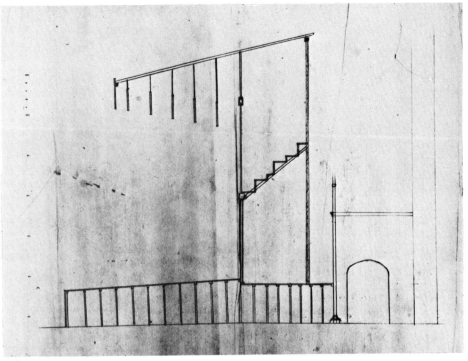

147

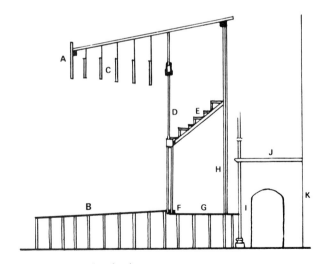

A Proscenium border
B Raked stage
C Cloud borders
D Shutter in grooves opening on the upper stage
E Upper stage area with tiered seats
F Shutter grooves at stage level
G Area of scenes of relieve
H The backcloth
I Hall screen
J Minstrel's gallery
K Wall of the hall

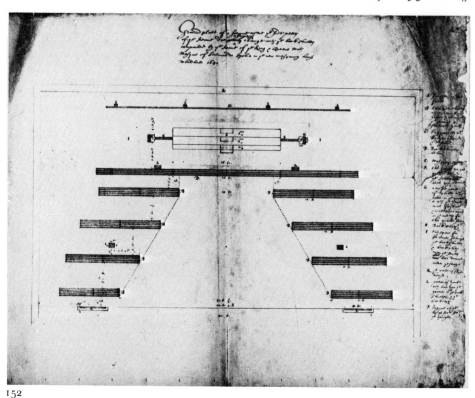

152

150 DIAGRAM OF THE STAGE for *Florimène* in action
O&S fig.105
Photograph

151 MODEL OF THE STAGE AND AUDITORIUM
Model maker: Mr Philip Wood

These diagrams provide the best evidence we have about Jones's methods of producing plays with illusionistic settings. The hall of Whitehall Palace is arranged as for a masque (144), with the royal throne at the focal point of the perspective, and the rest of the audience ranged in tiers around three sides of the hall. The central area is left open, as much for the King's unimpeded view as for the dancing that concluded the entertainment. The setting consists of four pairs of angled side-wings (145, 146), which remained fixed, behind these two (or in the plan of the stage alone, three) back shutters, closed in the plan of the stage, open in the plan of the hall, and between these and the back cloth, three grooves for various arrangements of 'scenes of relieve', or cut-out settings. The side elevation (149, 150) shows the placement of the stage in relation to the architecture of the hall, with the minstrel's gallery and the screen behind the back cloth. The upper stage is arranged in narrow tiers; six cloud borders hang from the roof of the stage. It is interesting to observe that all the scene changes took place far behind the action. Jones in effect conceived his stage machinery as a unit separate from the fixed setting within which actors performed. (s.o.)

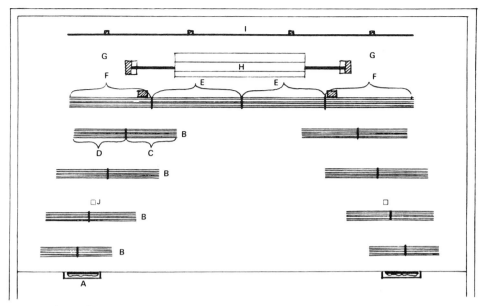

A Proscenium arch
B Side shutters
C Area occupied by side shutter when pushed on stage
D Area occupied by side shutter when withdrawn
E Area occupied by back shutter on stage

F Area occupied by back shutter when withdrawn
G Area for scenes of relieve
H The Queen's cloud machine
I The backcloth
J Pulleys for cloud machines

153

Sir William Davenant, *Salmacida Spolia*, 1640

John Webb (1611–1672) after Inigo Jones

152 GROUND PLAN OF THE STAGE AND SCENERY
B. M. Lansdowne MS 1171, fol.3I–4   O&S 399; S&B 321
Photograph

153 DIAGRAM OF THE GROUND PLAN of *Salmacida Spolia*
O&S fig.118
Photograph

John Webb (1611–1672) after Inigo Jones

154 ELEVATION OF THE STAGE
B. M. Lansdowne MS 1171, fol.1b–2   O&S 400; S&B 322
Photograph

155 DIAGRAM OF THE ARRIVAL OF THE GREAT CLOUD in *Salmacida Spolia*
O&S fig.119
Photograph

156 DIAGRAM OF THE ELEVATION OF THE STAGE in *Salmacida Spolia*
O&S fig.120
Photograph

157 MODEL OF THE STAGE for *Salmacida Spolia*
Model maker: Mr Bruce Rowling, Thurloe Models Ltd

158

It is easy to see from these plans how different the masque stage was from that of the drama. *Florimène* has a standing scene with angled side wings, and all changes of setting take place behind the action. For *Salmacida Spolia* the stage is much shallower, and movable settings extend forward to the proscenium. In a masque, the changes of setting actually are the action. There are four pairs of side wings (152), each consisting of four shutters, three sets of back shutters, and between these and the back cloth a complex arrangement of scenes of relieve. The side elevation (154) shows how elaborate was the relation between changes on the upper and lower parts of the stage, and indicates the position of engines for ascents and descents. (s.o.)

158 FOUR ROUGH SKETCHES for an Unknown Masque of 1621
Pen and black ink: 19·8 × 22·7 O&S III verso; S&B 395
The Trustees of the Chatsworth Settlement

159

On the reverse of a woodland scene probably prepared for a lost masque of 1621 appear four rough sketches. The first, at the upper left, is the earliest plan of perspective scenery in the history of the English stage. It demonstrates that the highly sophisticated scenic machine of *Salmacida Spolia* and *Florimène* was already in use in the Jacobean masques. The two drawings below represent rough versions of the pastoral setting on the recto: two deities descend in clouds on the left, and a more detailed scene of cloud-borne figures appears on the right. In 1632, Jones was to describe the masque as 'nothing else but pictures with light and motion'. These sketches show him thinking out the concept, a radical one in the English theatre, over a decade earlier. (s.o.)

Sir William Davenant, *Salmacida Spolia*, 1640

159 REWORKING OF SALMACIDA SPOLIA
Pen and brown ink: 24·8 × 18·8 o&s 415; s&b 351
The Trustees of the Chatsworth Settlement

First performed on January 21st, 1640, this is a sketch for a subsequent performance of *Salmacida Spolia*, without the Queen who was *enceinte*. A second performance of the masque was staged in February, and the Queen did dance in it; but Henrietta Maria was enduring a difficult pregnancy, and Jones apparently considered the possibility of restaging the entertainment without her. This schematic drawing shows actors and singers in position on stage. The personnel differs from that of the first production (the great cloud, according to Jones's notes, contains 'musitians' rather than lady masquers) but both the date and the subject matter clearly relate the design to *Salmacida Spolia*. The drawing also reveals how detailed Jones's thinking was about the staging of his productions, and how completely integrated actors and musicians were with the scenic picture. (s.o.)

William Habington, *The Queen of Aragon or Cleodora*, 1640

160 SCENERY FOR AN UNIDENTIFIED PLAY IN THE COCKPIT, 1639, OR AN ABANDONED PROJECT
for *The Queen of Aragon or Cleodora*
Pen and brown ink: 22·1 × 19 O&S 443; S&B 361
The Trustees of the Chatsworth Settlement

One of Jones's rare sketches indicating scenic structure: masking cloud borders, tent side wings, both upper and lower stage shutters withdrawn, the lower revealing a *citti of rileve*, the upper the 'backcloth' of clouds. The note 'for the cokpitt for my Lord Chamberlin' must refer to the Earl of Pembroke, who on April 10th, 1640, presented *The Queen of Aragon, or Cleodora* before the King and Queen at his own expense in the Hall of Whitehall Palace. This should be a project for presenting it in the Cockpit, subsequently abandoned. Objections by scholars that it cannot possibly be for the Cockpit because of its shape ignore Jones's ability to insert a stage of whatever the design he chose into any given area. (R.S.)

Machines

Sir William Davenant, *Luminalia*, 1638

161 SCENE 4: CLOUD SCENE
Design for a cloud machine
Pen and brown ink: 19·4 × 18·9 O&S 387; S&B 382
The Trustees of the Chatsworth Settlement

162 DIAGRAM OF THE FINAL SCENE in *Luminalia*
O&S fig.116
Photograph

Luminalia was Jones's most elaborate aerial spectacle, and made striking use of the mechanics of the fly-gallery, which he had introduced at the beginning of the decade. The masque included not only the usual flying chariots, but also complex cloud effects revealing a whole city supported on a rainbow, and the final epiphany of 'a heaven full of deities', consisting of a full musical consort and a chorus. (S.O.)

Ben Jonson, *Love's Triumph through Callipolis*, 1631

163 VENUS
Design for a cloud machine
Pen and dark brown ink, squared with black lead for enlargement: 39·6 × 29·7
O&S 148; S&B 350
The Trustees of the Chatsworth Settlement

Love's Triumph through Callipolis was the earliest of Jones's productions to include a fly gallery, and it opened, for the first time in English theatrical history, with a curtain 'flying up' instead of falling to the floor or being drawn aside on a traverse. The fly gallery made possible a vastly more elaborate use of the heavens, and the number of ascents, descents, and aerial ballets increased enormously during the next decade. *Love's Triumph* concludes with the appearance of Venus in a cloud, which descends, deposits the enthroned goddess on earth, and then reascends without the throne. She is seen here seated within the machine; pencil lines indicate the battens upon which the device is constructed. (S.O.)

163

Aurelian Townshend, *Albion's Triumph*, 1632

164 INNOCENCEY, JUSTICE, RELIGION, AFFECTION TO THE COUNTRY AND CONCORD
Design for a cloud machine
Pen and brown ink: 19·6 × 18·5 O&S 209; S&B 311
The Trustees of the Chatsworth Settlement

After Charles and the masquers had danced the main masque of *Albion's Triumph*, the scene was transformed to 'a prospect of the King's Palace of Whitehall, and part of the city of London, seen afar off; and presently the whole heaven opened, and in a bright cloud were seen sitting five persons, representing Innocency, Justice, Religion, Affection to the Country, and Concord'. When these had descended, 'the cloud that bare them was in an instant turned into a richly adorned throne', (s.o.)

Sir William Davenant, *The Temple of Love*, 1635

165 CLOUD CONTAINING DIVINE POESY
Design for a cloud machine
Pen and brown ink over incised lines: 27·4 × 37·2 O&S 294; S&B 212
The Trustees of the Chatsworth Settlement

The drawing shows Divine Poesy in her cloud, together with the battens along which the device moved. The batten along which she would have descended to the ground was stationed normally behind the second pair of stage side wings. (R.S.)

91

166

Italian Prototypes

In 1589 the Grand Duke Ferdinand de' Medici, who had resigned from the Cardinalate the year before, married Christina of Lorraine, niece of the Queen of France, and the city of Florence celebrated the event with a month of festivities. The entertainment included six spectacular *intermezzi*, platonic allegories on the subject of the power of music. Costumes and scenic machinery were designed by Bernardo Buontalenti, the Medici court architect, and preserved and disseminated through engravings by Agostino Carracci and Epifanio d'Alfiano. These scenes demonstrate how completely Jones succeeded in domesticating the practice of Italian stagecraft. He studied Buontalenti's settings for the heavens, the underworld and the sea, and copied all of them for use in Caroline productions. This was for Jones a characteristic way of working. There is no evidence that he witnessed a single one of the many continental productions that he adapted or reworked. His sense of his material derived entirely from engravings and drawings, texts and descriptions. (s.o.)

Jacques Callot (1592–1635), *Teatro degli Uffizi*
166 INTERMEZZO: LA LIBERAZIONE DI TIRRENO, 1617
Engraving
Photograph

In 1586 Bernardo Buontalenti designed what was probably the earliest permanent theatre with movable perspectives and stage machinery in Europe, for the Palazzo degli Uffizi in Florence. It is shown here during a production given in 1617. From Callot's etching, it is obvious how directly Buontalenti adapted the form of the temporary masquing-hall stage to the court theatre. (s.o.)

167

Bernardo Buontalenti (1536–1608)
167 DESIGN FOR THE FIRST INTERMEZZO: THE HARMONY OF THE SPHERES
Pen and watercolour
Photograph

Epifanio d'Alfiano (*fl.*1591–1607) after Bernardo Buontalenti (1536–1608)
168 FOURTH INTERMEZZO: THE MUSIC OF HELL
Engraving
Photograph

Epifanio d'Alfiano (*fl.*1591–1607) after Bernardo Buontalenti (1536–1608)
169 FIFTH INTERMEZZO: THE MUSIC OF ARION
Engraving
Photograph

Part III: The King's Arcadia

Jones and Anne of Denmark: the last years

Jones was first professionally associated with Queen Anne, when the *Masque of Black-nesse* was performed on January 6th, 1605. He had probably been recommended to Anne of Denmark by her brother, King Christian. It is unlikely that Jones was concerned with any of the works on the Queen's Lodging at Greenwich carried out 1607–09, when Salomon de Caus laid out gardens, or in February 1614, when James I gave Greenwich to the Queen for life, for Simon Basil was still the Surveyor to the Works. In 1615 the situation was very different. Jones had now replaced the deceased Basil, and Queen Anne was ready to build. In this very year, Jones had refitted rooms in Arundel's own house at Greenwich, so he was at hand to provide the Queen with a startling solution to her problem of rebuilding an old gatehouse that spanned the public road between the palace precincts and the park. Although this H-shaped, 'House of Delight' or 'curious device' as Sir Dudley Carleton called it, is now one of the key facts of English architectural history, its genesis is not at all clear. In 1616 Jones had provided two designs, the first of which is unknown, and although the second design was proceeded with from October 1616, the building account was suddenly closed on April 30th, 1618, nearly a year before the Queen died of dropsy on March 22nd, 1619. We shall probably never know whether the first and second designs bore any relationship to the villa as completed in the 1630s for Queen Henrietta Maria. But there are hints, a copy of a design shows a plan of double cross shape, with porticoes on the north and south fronts, and the bridge across the road lit by a Palladian window – the first in an English country house. Eight years and an Italian journey after the inexperienced designs for Britain's Burse (28, 29), Jones has now emerged as a positive architect, and at the age of forty-three, one who could look forward to challenging the supremacy of continental architects.

In time for the splendid banquet given by the Queen for Pietro Contarini, the Venetian Ambassador in England, Jones effected some works at her palace at Oatlands. By June 1617 a 'greate gate' 'to ye vineyard' was to be the first of many sensitive reworkings of Serlian models. These gates (378–89) gave Jones much satisfaction. Often standing alone as entrances to gardens or courts, he could lavish much attention upon them, regarding them as exquisite small scale essays in architectural discipline. Perhaps the Queen liked them too, for the Great Gate is the central feature in the view of the palace, when Van Somer painted her portrait (174, 175) in 1617. If the Venetian Ambassador was taken hunting from Oatlands, there would have been a banquet at nearby Byfleet Lodge, where the two-storey classical portico drawn by John Aubrey (176) projected incongruously from the centre of the Elizabethan entrance front of the house. If this portico belongs to Queen Anne's brief tenure, then it was the most classical complete work that Jones had done to date, and the first portico in England. (J.H.)

170

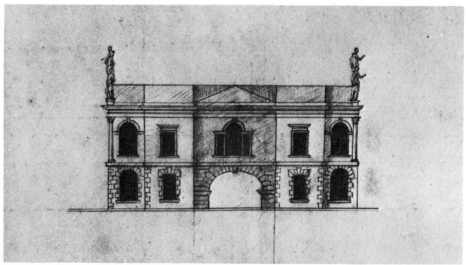

171

170 THE QUEEN'S HOUSE, GREENWICH
North elevation
Photograph

171 THE QUEEN'S HOUSE, GREENWICH
Copy of a design for the side elevations, perhaps the first project
Pen, pencil and wash: 32·6 × 42·9
The Provost and Fellows of Worcester College, Oxford

173   174

John Webb (1611–1672) after Inigo Jones

172 THE QUEEN'S HOUSE, GREENWICH
Plan, perhaps for the first or penultimate project
Photograph

Both drawings are copies made during the first half of the century, one as a theoretical or treatise study, the other a copy by Webb. The elevations of the Queen's House as built from *c.*1630, could hardly have resembled in detail what had been proposed, and begun in 1616. This is stylistically impossible, if we are to judge Jones's style then by the signed and dated 1616 elevation for the centre bay of an unidentified house (192). However, the copy of a design for the side elevations (171) is more sympathetic to this transition period. The rusticated windows and the loggias with arched openings, that project with full pediments on the north and south fronts, are motifs that seem early rather than late. Both plans must have been abandoned, for a painting of Charles I and his Queen in the park shows the plans of the incomplete building as it is today. However, the evidence from this painting, by Adrien Van Stalbemt and Jan Van Belcamp (d. 1653), should be treated with caution, as it is dated to *c.*1632 and therefore could show the Queen's House in process of completion, but not necessarily as begun. Without this painting, there seems to be no evidence that the plan as laid down in 1616 was the same as that completed from 1630. (J.H.)

173 OATLANDS PALACE, SURREY
Design for the Vineyard Gate
s: *Inigo Jones*: pen and pencil: 38 × 29
Royal Institute of British Architects

Following his return from Italy, Jones seemed to have signed his drawings, a habit

97

that ceases about 1620. Accompanying this design, there are in the RIBA collections two other drawings for the vineyard side of the gateway and for a gate 'that goith in to the Parke'. For the Vineyard Gate, Jones extemporised on Serlio; for the Park Gate, on Francart. In all, five gates were built. Henry, 9th Earl of Lincoln, a friend of Lord Burlington and William Kent, saved the Vineyard Gate from destruction, and had it rebuilt in 1735. Fragments are preserved in the Weybridge Museum. At the same time, 1616–1617, Jones designed an unidentified Silkworm House. (J.H.)

174 VINEYARD GATE, OATLANDS PALACE, SURREY
Detail of 175
Photograph

In front of the irregular and picturesque outline of the early palace is shown the Vineyard, which was entered by what is described in the accounts (P.R.O., A.O., roll 356, bundle 2487) as the 'Greate gate'. This record corresponds with the design in the RIBA made in 1616. (J.H.)

Paul van Somer (1577/8–1622)
175 ANNE OF DENMARK, 1617
Oil on canvas: 265·4 × 208·3
Her Majesty The Queen

Painted for Anne of Denmark and listed at Oatlands on October 7th, 1617. The painting also depicts Jones's classical gateway at her palace at Oatlands (174), completed the year the portrait was painted. As an image of the Queen, it reflects her ability to keep pace with aesthetic changes at court. It commemorates her patronage of the new architecture, of the chase and of a new type of royal portraiture. Van Somer was one of a series of Netherlandish painters, culminating in Van Dyck, whose robust style and muted baroque made the frigid icons of Larkin and De Critz outmoded. Anne is here glorified as the ideal lady *à la chasse* whose decisions are divinely guided: *LA MIA GRANDEZZA DAL ECCELSO* (R.S.)

John Aubrey (1626–1697)
176 BYFLEET LODGE, SURREY
View of the entrance courtyard
Photograph

The exact date of Byfleet's building is not known. It may be late Elizabethan, resembling Wimbledon Palace, but on a reduced scale, with shaped gables. It was granted to Henry, Prince of Wales in 1610, and to Queen Anne in 1616. A 'reparation' ordered in 1617 may not have included the astonishing classical portico, shown quite clearly in this sketch by Aubrey. If it was built for Queen Anne, it must rate with the classical frontispieces of Houghton Conquest. (J.H.)

Maximilian Colt (1596–1641)
177 HEAD FROM THE FUNERAL EFFIGY
Photograph

178

178 PROJECT FOR THE FUNERAL CATAFALQUE
Pen and brown ink: 30 × 18
Royal Institute of British Architects

Anne of Denmark died of dropsy on March 2nd, 1619. The funeral was delayed for lack of funds and did not take place until May 13th. Chamberlain' wrote to Carleton that the procession was 'a drawing tedious sight' and that the lords and ladies who walked in it 'made but a poor show'. Undoubtedly Jones's hearse in Westminster Abbey was the success of the day, 'the fairest and stateliest that I think was ever seen there'.

Jones's surviving design, which may not have been executed, is remarkable in that instead of depicting the usual recumbent effigy, it shows a seated figure, for which there was certainly no precedent in England. The effigy (177) for the hearse, of which the head still survives, was made by Maximilian Colt, and the decorative features on it were executed by John de Critz. Among the payments for the latter are those for a great lion and unicorn, and two wildmen to stand on the columns of the hearse, besides numerous coats of arms. There are references to 'a Crowne to sett on the top of the hearse' and freizes around it. (R.S.)

Arundel, Jones and the Italian Style

The acquisition of Palladio's drawings by Jones and those of Scamozzi by Lord Arundel, did not result in the transposition from the Veneto of a recognizably Palladian style. The implications of his climactic Italian journey took Jones a few years to assimilate and the years of 1615 to 1618 are a period of transition.

Not surprisingly, Lord Arundel was the first to employ Jones, on their return from Italy, and this was at his house in Greenwich, which may have been newly built by Jones. In a letter written c. April 1615, Arundel mentions gilt leather wainscot, the wainscot in the lower gallery and the removal of the organ to the lower dining room. What decorations Jones effected were burnt in January 1617. Jones's new-found Italianism can best be portrayed by this work at Arundel House c.1615–1619 and several designs and projects that seem to belong to the years immediately preceding the building of the Prince's Lodging at Newmarket (1619). Fortunately, the work on Arundel House was recorded by John Smythson, when he visited London in 1618-9. Regrettably, he seems not to have recorded all of Jones's interior features, for his drawings might have solved the problem as to whether the ground floor picture gallery and the upper floor sculpture gallery shown by Mytens, in his portrait of the *Earl of Arundel* (180) and referred to in August 1618, were arranged as depicted. These galleries may have been part of Jones's first important interior, an essay in sophisticated early *cinquecento* style.

Sir Fulke Greville's house at Holborn, recorded by Smythson (188), is almost certainly by Jones, with details strikingly similar to a design at Chatsworth (189), reminiscent of a whole group of building projects such as the Prince's Lodging at Newmarket, a country or town house (198), and most strikingly with parts of Raynham Hall c.1619–1622 (356). Most have balconies or 'pergulars' to their central windows and many have 'Dutch' gables of Venetian or northern derivation. The 'pergular' at Colonel Edward Cecil's house in the Strand was drawn by Smythson (190), and this can clearly be associated with a design by Jones. Perhaps the most perplexing drawing is the elevation for the central porch bay of a house of 1616 (192), Jones's first signed and dated drawing. One would like to associate it with Arundel, for he is the most likely patron in this year, and in a fascinating way it is still transitional, still the product of the Jacobean romantic.

The purity and simplicity of the Queen's House is held to be a major stepping stone to the designs for the Newmarket Lodging and Banqueting House but, of course, the Queen's House was not built in any recognizable form in 1616, so it cannot have acted as a catalyst. It is now clear that this Arundellian phase was transitional, and perhaps is no better displayed than in the frontispieces at Houghton Conquest (196–97) in Bedfordshire. This phase of Jones's style which occurs between 1615 and 1619 at the latest, was obviously of immense interest to metropolitan builders and architects, or those from the provinces, who came to London to see the latest fashions in architecture, witness John Smythson's topographical drawings. These lesser mortals were to make pedimented gables and pergulars *leit-motifs* of their subordinate style, which is loosely termed 'Artisan Mannerism', and derives far more from this phase in Jones's work than from his royal commissions, which were totally misunderstood by these subordinates.

179

Cornelis Bol (fl.*c*.1660)
179 VIEW OF THE THAMES WITH ARUNDEL HOUSE *c*.1640
Oil on canvas: 66 × 102·9
Trustees of the will of J. H. C. Evelyn deceased

This is the only detailed view of Arundel House, showing the Tudor north-south river wing, partially refaced and re-fenestrated by Jones, with the colonnade facing the west garden. For many years this colonnade sheltered some of the famous Arundel marbles. Unless this wing was rebuilt after 1620, it is difficult to locate some of the features recorded by Smythson, such as the 'new Italyan gate over the water' (185). The 'newe Italyan wyndowe' in the gallery could only have been on the east front of the wing, facing the parterre garden. With some artistic licence in the relationship of buildings, this garden is shown in the background of a portrait of Lord Arundel at Welbeck Abbey, attributed to Mytens. Near the river is shown a Jonesian garden gateway topped with three balls, like the park gateway at Oatlands of 1616. Hollar's engraved bird's eye view of the City, published *c*.1658, shows the physical relationship of the adjacent Somerset and Arundel Houses. He also engraved a view of the north-eastern courtyard of Arundel House which shows a building of six bays and two storeys with hipped roof and dormers. The simplicity and economy of this elevation can be likened to Lord Maltravers's design of 1638. It must be by Jones. (J.H.)

180

Daniel Mytens (*c.*1590–before 1648)

180 THOMAS HOWARD, EARL OF ARUNDEL, 1618
Photograph

In the background can be seen the Earl's sculpture gallery with his iron balcony over-looking the river.

John Smythson (d. 1634)

181 ARUNDEL HOUSE, THE ITALIAN GATE, 1619
Inscribed: *An Italyan gate in my Lo: of Arundelles garden: at London: at Arundell house*
See 182

182 HOUSE NEAR ROYAL EXCHANGE
Inscribed: *The fronte of house over agaynste the newe exchange*
Two drawings on one sheet; pen and pencil: 29·4 × 9·2
Royal Institute of British Architects

John Smythson (d.1634)

183 ARUNDEL HOUSE, CHIMNEY PIECE
Inscribed: *A chymnye peece at Arundelle House 1619*
Pen: 13·1 × 3·5
Royal Institute of British Architects

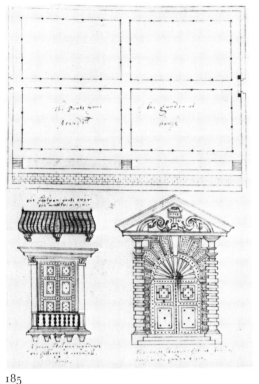

185

186

John Smythson (d.1634)

184 ARUNDEL HOUSE, PLAN AND ELEVATION OF AN ITALIAN WINDOW

Inscribed: *The uprighte draughte of the Italyan wyndowe at Arundell house* and *The grounde plate*

Pen and pencil: 21·1 × 15·2

Royal Institute of British Architects

John Smythson (d.1634)

185 ARUNDEL HOUSE, THE GARDEN PLATFORM, ITALIAN WATER GATE, ITALIAN WINDOW, ITALIAN GARDEN GATE

Inscribed: *The Plateforme of the garden at Arendell house* and *the Italyan grate over the watter* and *a newe Italyan wyndowe the gallerye at arrundell house* and *The newe Italyan gate at Arundell house in the garden there*

Pen and pencil: 27·9 × 19

Royal Institute of British Architects

186 ARUNDEL HOUSE, THE NEW ITALIAN GATE

Inscribed: *design for the newe Italyan gate*

Pen and wash: 44 × 37

Royal Institute of British Architects

John Smythson's drawings of the latest *Italyan* architecture in London, made on a visit there 1618–1619, are precious architectural documents. Clearly, he was interested in this important phase of Jones's style, immediately after his Italian tour. The house *agaynste the new exchange* (182) is possibly by Simon Basil. In general Smythson's draw-

gụ̃ foulke gryuell: in houlbȯrnѵ

188

ings can be relied upon, but in detailed particulars they are inaccurate. The *newe Italyan gate*(186), nicely dated 1618, is shown with eleven blocks to the columns, whereas Jones's design shows four. There are also discrepancies between the *grate* (185) of the window overlooking the Thames and that shown in Myten's view of the sculpture gallery, which has a balcony with straight bars. Smythson's gallery window may have lit the gallery from the side. Topographically, Arundel House is sparsely documented, for there are few views which show these Italianate parts of Jones's improvements. Arundel probably commissioned work there from 1615, when Jones was simultaneously engaged upon his house at Greenwich. (J.H.)

187 DESIGN FOR A TEMPORARY DECORATION in the form of a pedimented archway with twisted columns, the spandrels ornamented with attributes of music.
Ink and wash: 24·1 × 8·7
The Trustees of the Chatsworth Settlement

It is not possible to date this drawing closer than *c*.1610–*c*.1620. It is obviously for Arundel House. The twisted column is known as the Salomonic type, and it is notable, that a primary source is Lafreri's *Speculum Romanae Magnificentiae*, which has one plate devoted to the column in St Peter's, Rome. Twisted columns were proposed by Isaac de Caus at Wilton Garden in the mid-1630s, and to this period also belongs the porch of St Mary's, Oxford (1637) by Nicholas Stone, and Sir Thomas Gorges' monument of 1635 in Salisbury Cathedral. (J.H.)

189

John Smythson (d.1634)

188 FULKE GREVILLE'S HOUSE IN HOLBORN ADJACENT TO BATH HOUSE
Inscribed: *Sur foulke gryvelles in houlborne 1619*
Pen and coloured inks: 16·5 × 17·8
Royal Institute of British Architects

Although this house cannot be matched accurately to any design by Jones, there are
sufficient similarities to the design at Chatsworth to suggest that it is in fact by Jones.
(J.H.)

189 PROBABLY FULKE GREVILLE'S HOUSE, WITH A CENTRAL BALCONY AND A SCROLLED
PEDIMENTED GABLE
Pen and wash: 42·1 × 25·5 Chiswick 19
The Trustees of the Chatsworth Settlement

In time this design belongs to the period *c.*1617–*c.*1620. Its keyed windows may be
compared to those on the sheet of windows dated April 1618 (193), to the Newmarket
designs of 1619 (204–5), and particularly to what was being worked out for Raynham
Hall from 1619 (356). Fulke Greville's house was originally Hankford House and later
became known as Bath House. Greville, created Lord Brooke in 1620, may have
contemplated a new house on this site, but subsequently was content to add to one
side of the existing building, and may also possibly at the same time have formalized
the old front with a more regular pattern of windows and projecting oriels. (J.H.)

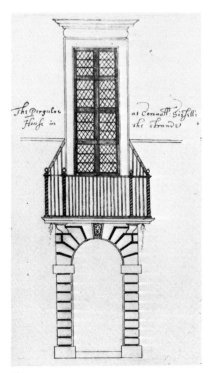

190   191

John Smythson (d.1634)

190 COLONEL SIR EDWARD CECIL'S HOUSE IN THE STRAND
Inscribed: *The Pergular at Coronall Sissell's House in the strande*
Pen and wash: 24·1 × 14
Royal Institute of British Architects

Cecil was Keeper of Putney Park and a relation of both Sir Fulke Greville and Robert Cecil, Earl of Salisbury and with Jones and Arundel a witness to the Deed of Foundation of Dulwich College in 1618. The balcony and the arched doorway beneath are perfectly matched by Jones's design (191). (J.H.)

191 COLONEL SIR EDWARD CECIL'S HOUSE IN THE STRAND
Inscribed: *Pergular*
Pen and wash: 48 × 36
Royal Institute of British Architects

Here Jones purloined a design from the recently published *Livre d'Architecture* by Francart of 1616. (J.H.)

192 UNIDENTIFIED ENTRANCE TO A HOUSE
Signed and dated: *Inigo Jones 1616*
Pen and wash: 35·5 × 31
Royal Institute of British Architects

This is the earliest documented design made by Jones after he returned from Italy. The project remains tantalisingly unidentified, but one would at this early date conclude the patronage to emanate from the Arundel or Cecil families. The emphasis

192

upon the single bay, at the expense of the adjacent wall elevation, suggests that this is an addition or frontispiece to an earlier house. The height from ground to balustrade is 44 feet. It is tempting to limit it to work at one of Arundel's houses, perhaps Greenwich or Ashurst, in Highgate, but it should also be remembered that Jones was working by June 1615 at Pishiobury in Hertfordshire for Lionel Cranfield, Earl of Middlesex. This Earl was one of the select circle who attended Thomas Coryat's Philosophical Banquet in 1611, and may have employed Jones for more than this and the gateway of 1621 at Beaufort House in Chelsea (380–81). (J.H.)

193 THREE DESIGNS FOR VOUSSOIRED AND KEYSTONED WINDOWS, ONE DATED APRIL 1618
Pen, pencil and wash: 28 × 20
Royal Institute of British Architects

Voussoired windows of this type can be associated with the Chatsworth design (189) ascribed to Fulke Greville's house, and the Prince's Lodging at Newmarket, both of *c*.1618–1619. Although Jones is seeking here a metrical law for voussoirs and keystones, the dating of one sheet suggests that he was working out this problem with a particular building in mind. An elevation that remains unrecorded is the Marquis of Buckingham's Lodging begun in 1619; another would have been Jones's proposals for the Gallery elevation at Newmarket. (J.H.)

194 UNIDENTIFIED THEATRE
Plan and elevation
Pen and wash: 32·3 × 42·1
The Provost and Fellows of Worcester College

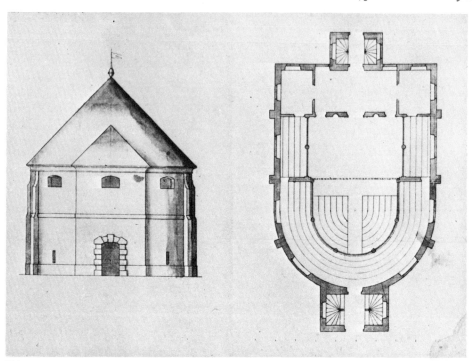

194

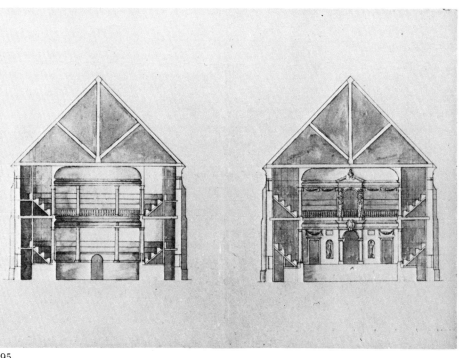

195

196

195 UNIDENTIFIED THEATRE
Sections
Pen and wash: 32·2 × 41·8
The Provost and Fellows of Worcester College

The proposed location of this project will long provide controversy. Stylistically it can be dated between *c.*1616 and *c.*1618. Its draughtsmanship is comparable to the design for Fulke Greville's house (189), which was built by 1619 at the very latest. It is not a royal commission, and if for a courtier, or produced under the patronage of a courtier, Lord Arundel is a likely candidate, especially in view of Arundel's friendship with Edward Alleyn. It is very tempting to associate this design with Alleyn's second Fortune Playhouse, which was rebuilt after a fire 1621–1622, but the style of drawing is too early. (J.H.)

196 HOUGHTON CONQUEST, BEDFORDSHIRE
Elevation of the north front measured·in 1785
Artist: W. Kimpton
Watercolour: 32·4 × 50·8
Trustees of the Bedford Settled Estates

197 HOUGHTON CONQUEST, BEDFORDSHIRE
Elevation of the west front measured in 1785
Artist: W. Kimpton
Watercolour: 32·4 × 50·8
Trustees of the Bedford Settled Estates

197

198

As mother of the 3rd and 4th Earls of Pembroke and a friend of Lord and Lady Arundel, Mary, Dowager Countess of Pembroke would have been likely to have employed Jones on her building works at Houghton Conquest from 1615, when she acquired Houghton, and before 1621, when she died. However, the house she built was fairly typical of the conservative court style of, for example, Simon Basil, except for two extraordinary classical frontispieces, one in the centre of the north front, and the other, a three-storey colonnade, on the west front. It is clear from an examination of the ruins that both belong to the main building programme and are not after-thoughts, for the west front carries the crests of Dudley and Sidney in the entablature. The remaining Doric ground storey shows the severely classical character of this super-imposed colonnade. From the north front, a three-bay, two-storey arched loggia pro-jected; a motif based on Palladio's Convento della Carita, crowned by a pedimented gable with ornamental parts that can be likened to Jones's design for St Paul's Cathedral of 1621. The addition of such classical appendages is reminiscent of the two-storey portico added to Byfleet Palace, also attributed to Jones. If such classical additions were made to Jacobean houses before 1621, then no one but Jones could have designed them. (J.H.)

198 DESIGN FOR A HOUSE WITH A PERGULA AND A PEDIMENTED GABLE
Pen and wash: 17·2 × 19·7
The Provost and Fellows of Worcester College

All the elements that make up this design belong to the Arundellian phase of Jones's practice. There is, once again, a comparison to be made with Raynham (356), where one of the entrances had an identical dropped lintel. (J.H.)

Surveyor to the Crown, Part I: 1615–1625

The history of the King's Works is a history principally of administration, the administering of building for the King, or indeed a Queen. It provides a continuous record from the medieval age to the present day, in the form of accounts, orders and letters in which the processes of commissioning building are documented. The method of artistic creation, and its transmission to the builder, is of lesser moment, because until Inigo Jones's Surveyorship, drawings were rare, and were few in relation to the buildings that must have been erected, even for those Jones administered or parcelled out to the various clerks and artificers.

Queen Elizabeth preferred her courtiers to build, so during her reign, the Office of Works spent no more than £4,000 per year. But under James I the Office became a power house of patronage; between 1607 and 1611 over £75,000 were spent. This was Stuart extravagance at its height and it was spent under Simon Basil's Surveyorship, not Jones's. His appointment to the Surveyorship coincided with a period of economy, and under these limitations Jones saw to it that his Office was run with efficiency and honesty, witness the comment that 'there was . . . scarcely any one Office in his Ma^ts Court of greater reputation both for able officers, good conduct, frugality of expence, and sure payment, than the office of his works'. Jones was a unique Surveyor. There had been none like him and as a Renaissance man of learning, a true *uomo universale*, he towered as a giant over the men under his command. Almost certainly this created a barrier between him and his staff, to whom he was an aloof courtier, intimate with the King and his great courtiers. He commanded no architect of remotely comparable stature; the best that could be mustered was Francis Carter, his Chief Clerk, and Nicholas Stone, head mason at the Banqueting House from 1619. It was through them and their colleagues, such as Edward Carter, that the Court style was diluted and transmitted to the country. Just how effectively Jones was able to transmit his commands through the administrative structure is difficult to assess, because so much has been destroyed. The links in this chain of command may well have been weak, and what, for example, Thomas Punter executed at the Prince's Lodging at Newmarket, in relationship to what Jones envisaged on the drawing board, may have varied considerably.

Much of Jones's work concerned humdrum tasks, the routine preparation of mansions for embassies, examination of sewers, flood control, the enforcement of building controls, and town planning commissions. When the history of the administration of architectural practice is written, Jones will feature considerably. Not all the royal works are accounted for in the Declared Accounts. Some, like the Banqueting House and the chapels at St James's and Somerset House, were accounted for separately, and many works for the Queens were paid for privately out of their Privy Purse accounts. The division between Jones as Surveyor, and Jones as a courtier architect, is a blurred one at the best of times. We shall never know the extent to which he delegated tasks within his command structure, nor how he used his own officers, when acting privately for courtiers. There is a growing body of evidence that he was an *eminence grise* to the success of many of his colleagues, none of whom, however, remotely understood the basis of his style. The group of royal buildings erected during his Surveyorship, under James I, were of seminal importance. In relationship to the comparatively small amount of monies expended, the influence of this phase of the Surveyorship was colossal, especially when seen as the nodal point for the spread of Neo-palladianism in the following century. However different the Prince's Lodging at Newmarket may have been from the two designs, they adumbrate the English Caroline country house in its maturity; or the design for the Lodge in Hyde Park is the source and epitome of the 18th century English villa. In nearly every work by Jones, a classical precedent is established for a whole or a part of English architectural composition. Perfect standards were set for the grammar of architecture and ornament. With the designing of James I's catafalque, for his funeral in Westminster Abbey in 1625, this phase of patronage came to an end, and it was the end also of large scale building for the Crown. (J.H.)

Works executed under the Surveyorship 1615–1625

1615–1617 Newmarket brewhouse, stable, dog house and riding house; stables for Sir Thomas Compton and Mr Duppa

1616–1618 Greenwich, The Queen's House

1617–1618 St James's Palace, the Prince's Buttery
Somerset House, lantern over the hall
Oatlands Palace, the park and vineyard gateways, probably three other gateways, and the silkworm room

1619 Hearse for Queen Anne's funeral

1619–1620 The Marquess of Buckingham's Second Lodging at Whitehall

1619–1621 The Prince's Lodging and Clerk of Works' house at Newmarket

1619–1622 The Banqueting House, Whitehall

1620–1621 Additions to the Countess of Buckingham's Lodging, Whitehall

1623–1624 New ceiling for the House of Lords, Westminster
Stables at Theobalds Palace

1623–1625 The Queen's Chapel at St James's
Remodelling of the Elizabethan chapel at Greenwich Palace and Great Gate in the park there

1624 Park stairs at Whitehall Palace

1625 Banqueting House at Theobalds Palace
Alterations to Dover Castle
Catafalque for James I's funeral

Anonymous

199 WILLIAM PORTINGTON
Oil on panel: 104·2 × 86·3
The Worshipful Company of Carpenters, London

William Portington held the office of Master Carpenter in the Office of Works from 1595 to 1629. As such he was a member of the Board and a colleague of Inigo Jones. In 1608 he executed the very complicated stage machinery for Ben Jonson's *Masque of Beauty*, when it was performed in the old Banqueting House at Whitehall, and in 1619 he was one of the Officers of the Works who signed the estimate for building the existing Banqueting House. He died in March 1629 (not 1628 as stated on the portrait) and was buried at St Martin's in the Fields. (H.M.C.)

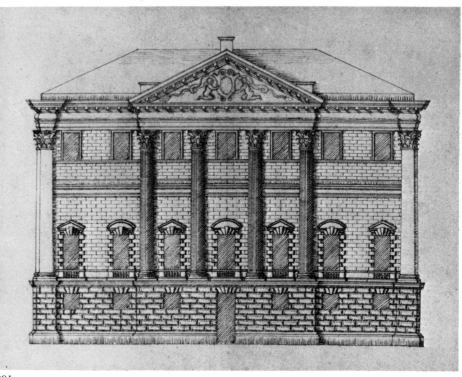

201

John Webb (1611–1672) after Inigo Jones

200 STAR CHAMBER
Plan of ground floor showing compartition of ceiling
Pen and pencil: 35·5 × 45
The Provost and Fellows of Worcester College

John Webb (1611–1672) after Inigo Jones

201 STAR CHAMBER
Elevation of one porticoed front
Pen and pencil: 35·5 × 45
The Provost and Fellows of Worcester College

John Webb (1611–1672) after Inigo Jones

202 STAR CHAMBER
Longitudinal section
Pen and pencil: 35·5 × 45
The Provost and Fellows of Worcester College

?Inigo Jones

203 DESIGN BASED ON STAR CHAMBER SECTION showing the addition to one side of another debating chamber.
Inscribed by John Webb: *upright for H. of C.*
Pen and pencil: 34·1 × 40·1
The Trustees of the Chatsworth Settlement

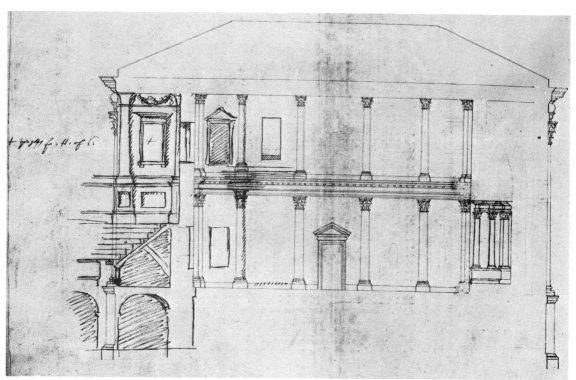

203

From medieval times the Star Chamber was where the King's Council met and it was so called *camera stellata* or *chambre des estoiles*, because in the fourteenth century it was decorated with gilded stars. It was sited in New Palace Yard, Westminster, and was rebuilt in 1602. In Worcester College are also (location no. HT 1–2) Jones's designs for the plan, which corresponds to Webb's copy above (200). This plan Jones dated 1617, the year John Chamberlain wrote on June 22nd to Sir Dudley Carleton that 'the King would fain have built' a Star Chamber 'if there were money'. Jones's design was created as a symbol and reflection of the King's justice, of James as the modern Solomon. As King in Council, he would adjudicate from the great niche. As Dr. Per Palme has so succinctly stated, 'Inigo Jones's model for the Star Chamber was an inspired amalgam of three prototypes, the traditional English hall with high walls and light from above, the ancient and modern basilicas with their associations to the judicature and to solemn rites, and finally two Roman temples dedicated to Sol and Jupiter, the two deities which in the Stuart Age were time and time again cited as allegorical personifications of the sovereign, the crowned image of God, the very source of Justice. This compound... was carried over into the conception of the Banqueting House'. The Chatsworth design (203), preserved among those for White-hall Palace, is perplexing as 'H of C' must surely mean House of Commons. Was there then some plan to amalgamate a new Star Chamber with a new Commons? In the old Palace the two chambers did not adjoin. Webb's copies of the Star Chamber designs were made after 1628, when he entered Jones's employment. However, it is unlikely that Jones would have resurrected the Star Chamber project as late as this. Therefore the idea of conjoining two chambers must be before 1628, and probably before 1620.

(J.H.)

204

204 NEWMARKET PALACE, THE PRINCE'S LODGING
Elevation for an astylar front
Pen and wash: 19·5 × 28
Royal Institute of British Architects

205 NEWMARKET PALACE, THE PRINCE'S LODGING
Elevation for a porticoed front
Pen and wash: 19 × 27·5
Royal Institute of British Architects

206 NEWMARKET PALACE, THE BREWHOUSE AND PRINCE'S GALLERY
Details of windows of the Brewhouse, and probably of the Prince's Gallery
Photograph

207 NEWMARKET PALACE, THE BREWHOUSE
Plan and elevation
Signed: *Inigo Jones*
Pen and wash: 38·5 × 22
Royal Institute of British Architects

208 NEWMARKET PALACE, THE STABLE
Elevation
Pen and watercolour: 32 × 41
Royal Institute of British Architects

Lacking topographical documents, exactly what was built at Newmarket will never be known. What is known, however, is that these designs were not executed as drawn. Both the Brewhouse and the Stable were built 1616–1617, following the building of a new block of lodgings 1614–1615, possibly Simon Basil's last work. In the accounts (P.R.O., E 351/3251) the stable is described as 'a faire lardge newe Stable for

205

greate horses' and measured 116 by 40 feet; the Brew House measured 82 by 60 feet (P.R.O., E 351/3251–2) and there was also a Dog House (P.R.O., E 351/3252). Jones designed stables for Sir Thomas Compton and Mr. Duppa 1617–1618 (P.R.O., E 351/ 3252). In 1619 the Prince's Lodging was put in hand (P.R.O., E 351/3253), but what the accounts reveal is probably a severely reduced version of Jones's astylar design, but of only five windows across the front. There was, however, a long rear addition called the Prince's Gallery, for which there survives a drawing of a window (206), and this may have contained a hall of double cube proportions. The Tuscan order of the Brew-house, again Scamozzian, is a forecast of what was to come at St Paul's Covent Garden. It is possible, that in these early years of his Surveyorship, Jones initially designed buildings on an ideal plane, rather than one geared to the economics of the Exchequer. (J.H.)

209 THE BANQUETING HOUSE
Main elevation
Photograph

210 THE BANQUETING HOUSE
Plan and elevation of the first (known) design
Pen, pencil and wash: 57·3 × 43·6
The Trustees of the Chatsworth Settlement

211 THE BANQUETING HOUSE
Plan of the basement, properly ground, storey of the second design
Pen and wash: 57 × 34
Royal Institute of British Architects

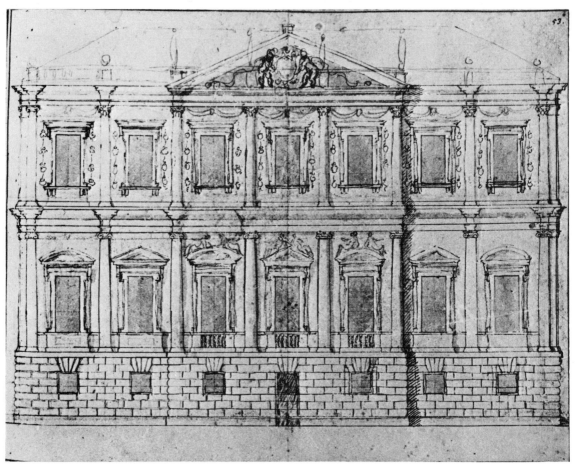

212

212 THE BANQUETING HOUSE
Elevation of the penultimate façade design
Pen and wash: 36·3 × 43·8
The Trustees of the Chatsworth Settlement

213 THE BANQUETING HOUSE
Elevation of the Great Door
Inscribed and dated by Jones 1619
Pen and pencil: 55 × 35·5
Royal Institute of British Architects

214 THE BANQUETING HOUSE
Preliminary design for one of the upper windows of the front
Pen and pencil: 24·5 × 15·5
Royal Institute of British Architects

The first Banqueting House in Whitehall was designed by Thomas Graves in 1581. It was of timber with canvas walls painted 'with a worke called rustike, much like to stone', but it could have hardly been classical. It was succeeded early in 1606 by a new

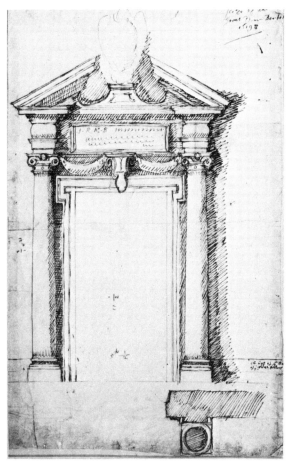

213

(second) building, which was drawn in plan by Robert Smythson in 1609. With the aid of this plan, and contemporary descriptions, it was an interior measuring 120 by 53 feet, with galleries of Ionic columns superimposed over Doric, and was obviously adapted from the idea of a Roman basilica, an astonishingly advanced notion for 1606. The idea of a classical Roman precedent for a masquing room had been initiated. It seems hardly unlikely that Jones, the prince of masque designers, was not consulted. However, in 1607 its author was referred to as 'Ld Architect', and this is interpreted to mean Sir David Conyngham, the King's Master of the Works in Scotland. On January 12th, 1619, the hall was destroyed by fire and its rebuilding was imperative. Jones produced designs and estimates by April 19th, building accounts opened on June 1st, and the building was complete, when these accounts closed on March 31st, 1622. Preliminary drawings at Chatsworth and the RIBA show how Jones arrived at his final solution of plan and elevation. From the first, he had in mind a Roman basilica, by Palladio out of Vitruvius, and he prefaced this room with ante-chambers at each end, not based upon a classical prototype, but given authority by the plan he had devised for the Star Chamber in 1617, and like the Chamber, incorporating a great niche at one end of the hall. The measure of the basilical space remained constant, a double cube 110 by 55 feet, although this had to be manipulated slightly to solve a problem concerning the distribution of the orders. Jones had to relate this longitudinal basilica with a main frontal elevation, a contradiction in classical terms because a basilica should be entered from one end. In the first Chatsworth elevation (210), which is as much Scamozzian as Palladian in derivation, there is no attempt to eliminate this contradiction, although its function as a side elevation is proclaimed by its lack of an entrance. It has a decided central emphasis of a two-storey attached portico of half columns. In the RIBA plan of the vaulted crypt or ground floor (211), the order throughout is a pilastered one, a sign that Jones was moving towards the idea of eliminating the central accent, but in the second Chatsworth design (212), Jones hesitates between this duality, for although he retains the attached half columnated portico and even gives it added emphasis by the entrance in the rusticated basement, in tentative outline, the final solution of eliminating the pediment altogether is anticipated. As Jones's mind worked upon this evolutionary sequence of changes, so he drew away further and further from his Vicentine prototypes. The Banqueting House as built has lost the tensions of Palladio's town house façades and has aquired serenity of proportions. It is very much an understated essay.

It is possible that he intended the Banqueting House to be flanked by some form of supporting structures, for as Hollar shows, the outside staircase on its north end looked temporary. Apart from the windows, some of which were always blocked, and all of which had the seventeenth-century mullion and transom of the Arundel House type, the Banqueting House looks today very much as completed in 1622 – except for one important fact: it is now all faced with Portland stone, a process which was begun by Sir William Chambers and completed by Sir John Soane. In the seventeenth century its basement was of honey-coloured Oxfordshire stone, the upper walls of a brownish Northamptonshire stone, and white Portland for the enriched details. It was a subtle essay in the art of polychromy, an effect of which can be recaptured by the pavilions of Stoke Bruerne. If the interior today looks Neo-classical in the late eighteenth-century style, it is due to the recurrent restorations, especially that by Sir Robert Smirke in 1837. Probably before 1630, it had lost its *great Neech*, coffered like the apse of the Temple of Venus and Rome as restored by Palladio, and the *Great Doure* (213) for which there is such a splendid design dated 1619, may not have been executed, as a single splendid door like this to face the royal presence enthroned under the great niche, is not mentioned in the accounts. The unfortunate break in the balustrade at the north end was made by Smirke who installed an organ here. The great crypt, really a ground floor undercroft, was often used as a place to take wine. Here in 1623–1624 Isaac de Caus built an elaborate grotto or 'rocke' costing £20, to which in 1625–1626 he added ten pounds worth of 'shell worke'. The grotto he constructed at Woburn ten years later survives as a good example of the lost Banqueting House one. (J.H.)

Peter Paul Rubens (1588–1640)

215 THE WHITEHALL BANQUETING HOUSE CEILING
Photograph

The ceiling panels by Rubens were Jones's master touch to the conception of the Banqueting House as a ceremonial hall and *salle des fêtes*. Rubens had been approached as long ago as 1621 concerning the Whitehall Banqueting House, but it was not until after his visit to England in 1629–1630, that any progress seems to have been made and they were not finally placed in position until 1635. Then Jones seems to have made a

215   216

major error, for he had not taken into account the harm of the torch light from the masques, so that when masquing resumed in 1638, it was in a temporary masquing hall built in the courtyard next to the Banqueting House.

From the start Jones must have been intimately associated with the project for the ceiling, in which the principles expressed in the masques found permanent expression in the pattern of ideas in paint, hovering over the heads of the court. The theme of the Banqueting House ceiling, rich and recondite in detail, may be summed up as a glorification of the earthly deeds of a King by Divine Right and his reward at death epitomised in the central panel, where James I ascends into the empyrean. (R.S.)

Paul Van Somer (1576–1621)

216 JAMES I BEFORE THE WHITEHALL BANQUETING HOUSE
Oil on canvas: 226·1 × 149·2
Her Majesty The Queen

Probably painted *c.*1620, depicting James I standing before the Whitehall Banqueting House then under construction. The rendering of the building is accurate in some details, but uncertain in others. It reveals, however, the importance attached to the building by the Crown, as a symbol of the new ideals of the Stuart Court. James is placed in robes before the hall, in which he presided over the grandest of state ceremonies. (R.S.)

217 THE MARQUESS OF BUCKINGHAM'S SECOND LODGING IN WHITEHALL, DINING-ROOM CEILING
Plan of four coves and section through cornice, painted with arms of Villiers impaling Manners and the motto *Fidei Coticula Crux*
Pen, pencil and watercolour: 28·5 × 31·1
The Provost and Fellows of Worcester College

217

The arms on this beautiful drawing refer to the marriage of the Marquess of Buckingham to Lady Katherine Manners on May 16th, 1620. In 1619 the Office of Works were paying for the Marquess's new or second lodging, which was probably a large house or frontage adjacent to the King Street Gate, where the Duke's mother had a Lodging. In the Parliamentary Survey of 1650 the 'large and Comely roome called the Dyninge Roome' is singled out for especial praise, and this is the dining room whose ceiling was accounted for September 30th, 1620 (P.R.O., E 351/3243). The archaeological derivation of this ceiling is from Palladio's illustration of the Temple of Neptune, and it can be compared to the classical coffering in the Queen's Chapel at St James, and the House of Lords, both being built in 1623. However, it is not entirely certain that this ceiling is for Whitehall, for by 1622 Jones was involved in considerable interior works for Buckingham at New Hall in Essex, and we know nothing about the interiors of the Duke's splendid house at Burley-on-the-Hill, Rutland, also being altered at this time. (J.H.)

Daniel Mytens (*c.*1590–1648) and Hendrik van Steenwyck (*c.*1580–*c.*1648)
218 GEORGE VILLIERS, 1ST DUKE OF BUCKINGHAM (1592–1628), 1626
Oil on canvas: 240 × 132·1
The Duke of Grafton, Euston Hall

The portrait was painted for Charles I and depicts Buckingham at the age of twenty-four. The perspective in the background shows an arcade close to that Jones designed for the masque *Time Vindicated* in 1623 (236). Both in turn may have been inspired by Hieronymous Cock's engravings of architectural perspectives by Vriedeman de Vries. (R.S.)

219

221

219 THE QUEEN'S CHAPEL, ST JAMES'S PALACE
View of the west front showing the original adjacent wing to the south, containing ante-rooms
Photograph

220 THE QUEEN'S CHAPEL, ST JAMES'S PALACE
View from the north-east showing reconstructed east end
Photograph

Johannes Kip (1653–1722)

221 THE QUEEN'S CHAPEL, ST JAMES'S PALACE
Engraving of the chapel fitted 1686–88 for Roman Catholic services as the domestic chapel of Mary of Modena, wife of James II
Photograph

222 THE QUEEN'S CHAPEL, ST. JAMES'S PALACE
Chimney piece in the Royal Closet
Pen and wash: 41 × 29
Royal Institute of British Architects

Initiated as a consequence of the proposed marriage between Prince Charles and the Spanish Infanta, the foundation stone was laid on May 16th, 1623, but building was eventually completed in May 1625, when Charles married Henrietta Maria. Despite many of the fittings, which date from after the Restoration, this chapel expresses more of the quintessential Jones than any other surviving building. Its west front is a trans-

224

position to a more monumental form of the centre section of one of the Newmarket designs, but the closest parallel to it, as a temple feature, is with the centre of the east front of Raynham Hall (356), another Newmarket derivative. The coffers in the ceiling of the Chapel are an imitation of those in Palladio's restoration of the Temple of Venus and Rome. Almost simultaneously, Jones was turning to his Serlio for coffers of a different kind in the great barrel-vault of the House of Lords. Today the east end has a Palladian window. This Palladian opening is shown in Kip's etched view of the interior in 1688, as an essential part of an illusionistic transparency, that was built here in the 1660s, when an apse was added. However, the Palladian window is almost certainly original to Jones's scheme, and in England was the prototype for a fashion that still has not died out. An early example was the old church of St John the Evangelist at

Stanmore, Middlesex, consecrated in 1632 by Archbishop Laud and with which Nicholas Stone seems to have been involved. (J.H.)

Wenceslaus Hollar (1607–1677)

223 THE HOUSE OF LORDS FITTED UP FOR THE TRIAL OF ARCHBISHOP LAUD 1644–1645
Engraving
Photograph

Peter Tillemans (1684–1734)

224 QUEENE ANNE IN THE HOUSE OF LORDS, painted between 1708 and 1714
Painting
Photograph

Exactly at the time Jones was designing the St James's Chapel, he reconstructed the House of Lords within the old medieval walls. The main problem was one of lighting the chamber, the walls of which were hung with the Armada tapestries. Jones ceiled the whole with a plaster barrel vault painted in *trompe-l'oeil* with imitation coffering, which is taken literally from Serlio's fourth book. It was, in effect, a larger scale version of the St. James's Chapel, but unlike the St James's ceiling, large square windows were cut into the vault. (J.H.)

Masques for Charles, Prince of Wales: 1616–1625

The Duke of York became the Prince of Wales in 1616, four years after the death of his idolised elder brother. Though there was a ceremonial *Barriers* to mark the event, on the whole Charles's creation was not celebrated with extraordinary festivities, and he did not dance in the Christmas masques of that year or the next. Possibly too much rejoicing would have seemed to King James to be tempting fate; the memory of Prince Henry was still fresh. But the character of the new Prince must also have proved an inhibiting factor; Charles was shy and introverted, with none of the exuberance and showmanship of his late brother. Indeed, it is fair to say that the festal spirit never really developed in him, and even during his reign, when he took the most intense interest in masques, he tended to treat them not as games or entertainments but as celebrations of his power and theophanic visions.

The Prince first led a masque on Twelfth Night 1618. Jonson's *Pleasure Reconciled to Virtue* is a fable about the education of a hero; Comus, god of sensuality and revelry, is banished by the moral fervour of Hercules, the prototype to the Renaissance of aristo-cratic virtue, who in his own youth had made the crucial choice between the goddesses of Pleasure and Virtue. In the masque, the example of Hercules is expounded by Mercury, god of philosophy, and Daedalus, the archetype artist; directed by these guides, Prince Charles and his knights appear and enter into a Whitehall chastened and admonished by Jonsonian moral exhortation. The court, however, proved unre-generate, and the masque was a dismal failure. The King interrupted the performance to complain angrily that there was too little dancing, and court correspondents clucked disapprovingly over the inappropriateness of poetical moralisings to the Prince's first masque. What was considered appropriate may be judged from the revised version of the masque, prepared by Jonson and Jones for a second performance six weeks later. Comus, his band and all the moral philosophy of Hercules and Mercury disappeared, to be replaced by a group of comic Welshmen and dancing goats.

Throughout the last years of King James's reign, low comedy remained a staple of the masque, always banished and superseded by the glorious visions of the royal peace. At the centre of these visions was Charles, Prince of Wales; in 1620 he danced the part of Truth in *News from the New World*, and of the Prince of Arcadia in *Pan's Anniversary*, performed on James's birthday. In 1622 he was Apollo's chief augur in *The Masque of Augurs* (232–234), and in 1623, in *Time Vindicated* (235, 236), Fame presented him as the leader of 'certain glories of the time'. For the final masque of the reign, the King as Neptune received his son as Albion, Prince of the Isles, descending from a floating island in *The Fortunate Isles and their Union* (237).

Jones's designs for these productions show a new sense of architectural solidity; and indeed, in at least two cases the settings represent actual buildings. The street scene (226) of *The Vision of Delight* could have been copied from any Italian handbook; it is a recognisable version of Serlio's standard settings of sixty years before. But *Time Vindicated* opens on a scene of Jones's own uncompleted Banqueting House (235), and its second scene appears to be based on an arcade that Jones had constructed for Buckingham. Similarly, the pastoral settings of 1621 show a new sense of depth and detail; Jones was now thinking of his stage pictures as realisations of a world. Nor were the fantastic visions lacking. The main setting of *Pleasure Reconciled to Virtue* (1618; no drawing survives) was a mountain with the head of an old man that rolled its eyes; and the extraordinary sketch of the Palace of Perfection (228) for a lost masque of the following year shows how elaborately co-ordinated Jones's apotheoses had become. (s.o.)

Daniel Mytens (*c*.1590–1648)
225 CHARLES I AS PRINCE OF WALES, 1623
Oil on canvas: 204·2 × 130
Her Majesty The Queen

The portrait is dated 1623 and is probably a version of the type commissioned to despatch to Spain in October, when the artist was paid £30 for a portrait of the Prince presented to the Spanish Ambassador. This is corroborated by the fact that it depicts Charles in dress cut on the lines of that worn at the Spanish court. (R.S.)

Ben Jonson, *The Vision of Delight*, January 6th and 19th, 1617
226 SCENE I: A STREET IN PERSPECTIVE
Pen and brown ink: 27 × 31·5 O&S 89; S&B 370
The Trustees of the Chatsworth Settlement

The earliest identifiable masque setting by Jones after his return from Italy. *The Vision of Delight* opens with 'a street in perspective of fair building', a setting Jones based on a combination of elements from two of Serlio's prototype settings (100,101). Charles did not take part in this masque, which was one of lords led by George Villiers, then Earl of Buckingham. The masquers were revealed in a bower as 'the glories of the spring', and the performance was notable for the first recorded use of dialogue sung as recitative. John Chamberlain described the reaction of the court to the masque: 'I have heard no great speach nor commendations of the mask neither before nor since'. (R.S.)

227

Ben Jonson, *Pleasure Reconciled to Virtue*, January 6th and 7th (with alterations as *For the Honour of Wales*) 1618

227 HERCULES, DAEDALUS AND MERCURY

Pen and brown ink washed with grey: 17·6 × 23·5 O&S 93; S&B 415

The Trustees of the Chatsworth Settlement

Pleasure Reconciled was the vehicle for Prince Charles's first appearance leading a court masque. As far as the court was concerned it was a disaster. Inigo Jones was reported to have 'lost his reputacion in reguard some extraordinary devise was loked for . . . and a poorer was never sene', and Jonson was castigated for having 'grown so dul that his devise is not worthy the relating, much lesse the copiing out'. This then was the reaction of the court to one of Jonson's and Jones's most perfectly constructed masques. That it was the inability of the English audience to understand the creation of both poet and designer is borne out by the long account by a Venetian observer, Orazio Busino, who is full of admiration for Jones's control of scenic spectacle. Atlas rolled his eyes and moved 'with wonderful cunning' and he describes how the mountain 'opened by the turning of two doors (presumably the parting of the lower stage back shutters), and from behind the low hills of a distant landscape one saw daybreak, some gilded columns being placed along the sides to make the distance seem greater (the side wings)'.

No designs survive for the scenery but there was clearly an upper and lower stage. Musicians sat in a tableau, probably in a scene of relieve, at stage level, and at the climax of the performance the masquers descended from the upper stage. The sketch (227) depicts the moment when Daedalus leads the masquers down from the hill while Hercules (left) questions Mercury (right). (R.S.)

228

Unknown Masque, January 6th, 1619
228 THE PALACE OF PERFECTION
Pen and brown ink washed with warm grey, incised with a point for enlargement:
37·5 × 30·8 O&S 100; S&B 301
The Trustees of the Chatsworth Settlement

Ben Jonson was in Scotland, when the Twelfth Night Masque for 1619 was performed.
'The maske was well liked and all things passed orderly' and it was 'superbly mounted
and proved a great success'. Prince Charles led the masquers in a spectacle, the text
and author of which remain unidentified. The association of the drawing for the
Palace of Perfection with this lost masque is only a tentative one. It certainly relates
to this period, when square proscenium arches were the norm, and repeats the scenic
arrangements of *Pleasure Reconciled* with, presumably, musicians in tableau at stage
level and an upper stage vision from which the masquers descended down the staircases,
past the heroic statues, in the same way that they were led down Mount Atlas. Shortly
after this masque the Whitehall Banqueting House was burnt down. (R.S.)

230

Ben Jonson, *Paris Anniversary, or the Shepherds' Holiday,* June 19th, 1620

229 ? SCENE I: ARCADIA

Pen and brown ink washed with grey: 38·5 × 33·9 O&S 109; S&B 386

The Trustees of the Chatsworth Settlement

The masque was presented by Prince Charles and the lords, in honour of James I's birthday at Greenwich Palace. It was not a complicated spectacle. There were only two scenes, the first being Arcadia, which subsequently opened to reveal 'the masquers sitting around the fountain of light'. The set was square, the norm for this period, being 38 by 38 feet. This drawing is also a rare record of stage construction, recording the appearance of the stage with the stairs either side leading down from the upper stage indicated, but minus the side wings, which would have masked them. (R.S.)

Unknown Masque, January 6th and February 11th, 1621

230 PROSCENIUM AND HUNT SCENE

Proscenium in pen and black ink, the scene in pen and brown ink washed with sepia, squared with a point and black lead for enlargement and splashed with scene-painters' brown distemper: 44·5 × 46·2 O&S 110; S&B 400

The Trustees of the Chatsworth Settlement

231

Little is known of the masque for Twelfth Night 1621. It presumably took place in the hall of Whitehall Palace as the new Banqueting House was under construction. Recorded as having been 'handsomly performed', it shocked some by openly flouting a Puritan on stage. The association of this drawing with the masque for 1621 is only tentative, reached by stylistic comparison (*cf.* the trees in *Pan's Anniversary*, 229) and by the fact that its contents fit none of the Jonson masques. In the sky there is a circle, inscribed in lead, indicating an opening at upper stage level for celestial tableau, as in the *Masque of the Augurs* the following year (232). Two other drawings relate to this masque, on the reverse of one, there is a highly important ground plan of the scenery together with sketches of the masque in action (158). No.230 is one of the largest and most beautiful of all Jones's scenic designs. (R.S.)

*Unknown Masque, c.*1619–23

231 CUPID'S PALACE

Pen and brown ink squared for transference: 53·3 × 43·8 O&S 113; S&B 405
The Trustees of the Chatsworth Settlement

No masque for which records survive refers to Cupid's Palace, although the design could conceivably relate to the productions of 1619 and 1621, about which few details are known. The design can be dated closely to these years as it is similar to two build-

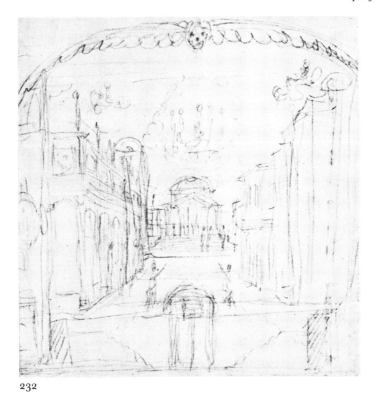

232

ings on which Jones was actually working. To the left, there is a building with a rusticated basement directly in the manner of the Whitehall Banqueting House and the
central palace is closely related to designs for Prince Charles's Lodging at Newmarket,
both under construction in 1619. A masque with the theme of the triumph of Cupid
would have been apposite for years when negotiations for Charles's marriage to the
Spanish Infanta were at their climax. (R.S.)

Ben Jonson, *The Masque of Augurs*, January 6th and May 6th, 1622

232 SCENE 2: THE COLLEGE OF AUGURS
Black lead: 23·1 × 19·7 o&s 115; s&b 63
The Trustees of the Chatsworth Settlement

233 APOLLO
Pen and brown ink: 20·2 × 26 o&s 116; s&b 411
The Trustees of the Chatsworth Settlement

234 ENTRY OF THE AUGURS PRECEDED BY THE POETS
Pen and brown ink washed with brown: 23 × 37·6 o&s 117; s&b 111
The Trustees of the Chatsworth Settlement

The Masque of Augurs inaugurated the new Banqueting House, and was devised jointly
by Jones and Jonson. It was the first time that Jones specifically placed a building of
his own design on stage, for the masque opened in the court buttery. Jonson used
the occasion for a pyrotechnic display of learning on the art of augury in classical
antiquity, while for Jones its seems to have been a vehicle for an architectural state-

234

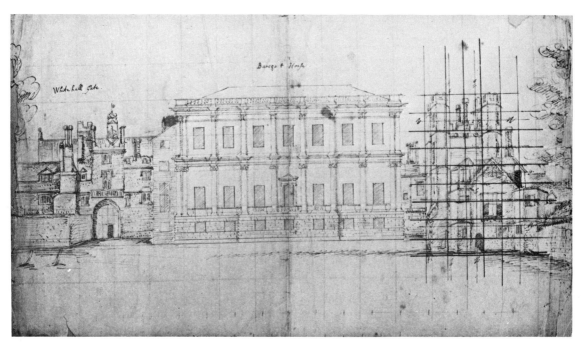

235

236

ment as if to emphasize the relationship of his stage buildings to the ones he was actually erecting. The important slight drawing in lead (232) shows the usual square proscenium, with a setting of classical buildings in perspective, leading to the College of Augurs, before which some of the masquers are indicated standing in tableau. Above there is a circular aperture revealing an upper stage tableau ('Jove, with the senate of the gods') flanked by two cloud machines, perhaps bearing Apollo (233), in two different positions, one for his arrival and the other for his departure. Two figures on stage are carrying augurs' staves.

The procession (234) is a rare document, showing people actually moving on stage. At the head walk two out of the four poets mentioned in the text, their heads garlanded with poetic bay leaves. The torchbearers are boys in antique dress, while the two augurs carry divining staves and wear cloaks which they would, presumably, have discarded for dancing. (R.S.)

Ben Jonson, *Time Vindicated to Himself and to His Honours*, January 19th, 1623

235 SCENE 1: WHITEHALL BANQUETING HOUSE
Photograph

236 PROSCENIUM AND SCENE 2: THE DISCOVERY OF THE MASQUERS
Pen and brown ink with incised lines marking the proscenium arch and a scale below: 37·3 × 46·6 O&S 123; S&B 198
The Trustees of the Chatsworth Settlement

The masque was led by Prince Charles and notable mostly for Jones's scenic spectacle which 'hath the whole commendation'. As in the *Masque of Augurs* the year before, it

237

239

opened with a specific building being placed on stage, this time the Whitehall Banqueting House (235), in its unfinished state with the improvised exterior staircase abutting the north end. The proscenium arch (236) had Time at the centre, flanked by the twelve zodiacal signs supported by the figures of Night and Day. Jonson's text is very cursory in its reference to scenic spectacle, but the masquers as the Glories of Time were presumably revealed in tableau at the end of the cloud-borne colonnade (236). (R.S.)

Ben Jonson, *Neptune's Triumph for the Return of Albion* (not performed) and *The Fortunate Isles, and their Union*, January 9th, 1625

237 THE FLOATING ISLAND OF MACARIA
Pen and brown ink washed with grey: 36 × 35 O&S 128; S&B 231
The Trustees of the Chatsworth Settlement

238 SCENE 3: THE HOUSE OF OCEANUS
Pen and brown ink washed with grey: 54 × 43·7 O&S 129; S&B 65
The Trustees of the Chatsworth Settlement

239 JOHPHIEL, MEREFOOL, SCOGAN AND SKELTON
Pen and brown ink: 22·5 × 19·2 O&S 130; S&B 66
The Trustees of the Chatsworth Settlement

Neptune's Triumph was planned for Twelfth Night 1624, but cancelled because of disputes over ambassadorial procedence. With some re-working, it was used for 1625 when the Venetian ambassador described it as 'a splendid masque, with much machinery and most beautiful scenery'. The masquers arrived on a floating island (237), a return to the moveable pageant cars of *The Masques of Blackness* and *Beauty*, on which Prince Charles sat as Albion surrounded by masquer lords. This was followed by two perspective scenes, one the House of Oceanus (238) and the second 'the

238

wonders of the deep', for which no design survives. The former is grotto architecture with a specific allusion to the creation of a grotto in the basement of the Banqueting House about 1624 by Isaac de Caus. Here again Jones is propagating the taste for the new Italianate garden, with mannerist marvels, by putting it on stage.

The costumes for the anti-masques (239) are an instance of where Jones's designs can disregard Jonson's text. The Airy Spirit to the left has no circlet of flowers on his head or silver fan in his hand. Merefool, the Rosicrucian, to the right, is not 'shrouded under an obscure cloak', nor is he fat. All these attributes are listed by Jonson in the text but ignored by Jones. (R.S.)

The Funeral of James I, 1625

240 DESIGN FOR THE HEARSE
Pen and brown ink washed with brown: 60·5 × 43·7
The Provost and Fellows of Worcester College

241 John Williams, *Great Britain's Solomon*, 1604
Frontispiece depicting the hearse
Photograph

242 ?DESIGN FOR A STUART MAUSOLEUM
Pen and brown ink washed with brown
The Provost and Fellows of Worcester College

James I died at Theobalds between eleven and twelve noon on the morning of March 27th, 1625. The corpse was immediately seared, wrapped in lead and laid within a sumptuous coffin. The new king appointed commissioners to organise the ceremonial of the funeral, a group which included the Earls of Arundel, Pembroke and Montgomery. These met at Whitehall on Tuesday March 29th, and gave orders for the corpse to be brought in state the following Monday to Denmark House. The procession which attended the body was in 'such manner as they do when the King removes', and arrived at Denmark House at 8 pm that evening. The coffin was laid on a catafalque in the lobby, beyond the Privy Chamber, surrounded by six candlesticks 'which King Charles had bought when he was in Spaine' with a canopy above. As in the case of Queen Anne, Maximilian Colt made an effigy to lie on the coffin. Colt had travelled to Theobalds 'for the moulding of the Kings face' and he apparently was called upon to make a second effigy 'suddenly to serve only att Denmarke house'. The body was made with joints, so it could be placed in 'severall postures' as life within Denmark House 'contynewed in all points as if his Majestie had been lyveinge'. On April 31st the coffin was moved into the Privy Chamber, the day after to the Presence Chamber and then followed a delay of two days, after which it was finally moved to the hall. The delay was due to Inigo Jones's hearse in Westminster Abbey not being ready. On May 7th, the funeral took place with some 9,000 persons in the cortège, including, which was a break with etiquette, the new king as chief mourner.

Inigo Jones's hearse (240) was reported as being 'the fairest and best fashioned that hath ben sen'. It consisted of a domed *tempietto*, covered with pennants and shields of arms and surrounded by statues of the virtues in attitudes of mourning. John Aubrey records being told by Emmanuel de Critz in 1649 that Jones 'made the 4 heades of the cariarides (which bore up the canopie) of playster of Paris, and made the drapery of them of white callico, which was very handsome and very cheap, and shewed as well as if they had been cutt of white marble'.

To this period belongs the drawing for a vast mausoleum in the antique manner (242), which is one of the strangest and most problematic of all Jones's architectural fantasies. A huge fortress, with a rusticated basement, bears a circular domed building with side chapels. The drawing is included here, the hypothesis being that it could relate to a project for creating a huge royal mausoleum. (R.S.)

240

242

Surveyor to the Crown, Part II: 1625—1640

Charles's reputation as a maecenas of the arts has disguised the fact that the Exchequer was in even more straitened circumstances than under his predecessor. The plans for rebuilding Whitehall Palace can be dated no earlier than 1638, but they have imparted to Charles's reign an aura of architectural grandiloquence. This was not so. Indeed, if one excludes the work carried out for Queen Henrietta Maria at Somerset House, Greenwich, Oatlands and Wimbledon, anything carried out directly for the King was in a minor key. Neither the Cockpit Theatre in Whitehall, nor the Lodge in Bagshot Park, nor the Hyde Park Lodge could be described as any more than small scale works. It was therefore natural that under this phase of the Surveyorship Jones should find time for public commissions. As the restoration of Old St Paul's Cathedral and the provision of a new screen at Winchester Cathedral were incumbent upon acts of royal piety, they were therefore marginally, but not directly, executed through the Office of Works. But they were still, nevertheless, in the private and public, rather than royal sector of Jones's career. During this time Jones continued to order the day to day business at the Office, arbitrating upon buildings, initiating surveys, discussing water supplies. From 1628 he had in his office as his personal assistant, John Webb. Gradually this amanuensis became as identified with Jones, as Hawksmoor was with Vanbrugh, and would carry the torch of Jones's Palladianism through the dark night of the Interregnum. A year after losing the Surveyorship in 1644, Jones was at the Sack of Basing House, and rather ingloriously was 'carried away in a blanket, having lost his cloaths'. The protean comet had burnt out in the sky. (J.H.)

Works executed under the Surveyorship 1625–1640

1625	Triumphal arch for marriage of Queen Henrietta Maria
1626	A clock house at Whitehall
	Queen's Cabinet Room at Somerset House
1627	Park gate at St James's
1628–1631	River stairs at Somerset House
1629	The Whitehall Cockpit
1629–1631	Queen's Withdrawing Chamber and pergula window and a sculpture gallery in the garden at St James's
1630–1635	The chapel at Somerset House
1630–1638	Completion and decoration of Queen's House at Greenwich
1631	A garden arbour at Oatlands Palace
	Park gate at St James's
1631–1632	Lodge in Bagshot Park
1632	The cistern at Somerset House
1634	A Lodge in Hyde Park
1635	A balcony at Oatlands Palace
1635–1636	Remodelling of the Cross Gallery at Somerset House
1636	Design for a chimney piece at Oatlands Palace
1637	A new masquing room at Whitehall
	A ceiling at Oatlands Palace
	The new Cabinet Room at Somerset House
1639	Alterations to Wimbledon House

243

Daniel Mytens (*c.*1590–1648)

243 CHARLES I, 1631
Oil on canvas: 216 × 134·6
The National Portrait Gallery (1246)

The portrait depicts Charles I in the year in which he danced in the first of the masques of the years of Personal Rule, *Love's Triumph through Callipolis,* and the year before Van Dyck's arrival in England. The portrait, of which there are several versions, captures admirably the mood of the King and of the new reign, subdued, elegant, aloof with the symbols of regal power, the crown, orb, and septre, to hand. (R.S.)

John Webb: 1611–1672

244 THE COCKPIT THEATRE AT WHITEHALL
Plan and section
Pen and brown ink: 35·5 × 45·4
The Provost and Fellows of Worcester College

Works Accounts show expenditure for the reconstruction of the old Cockpit as the Cockpit-in-Court Theatre, 1629–1631. Webb's plan and section could have been drawn in 1629 as he was then in Jones's office; however, the draughtsmanship is too mature, and as Dr. Per Palme has demonstrated, this drawing was made after 1660 when the Cockpit underwent certain repairs which included 'Ballisters upon the stage' and the addition of two chimneys (PRO Works 5/1 and 5/3). In early views of the exterior of the Cockpit no chimneys are shown, whereas they appear in Danckert's view of Whitehall *c.*1674. Webb's drawing may not be a working design, but one of

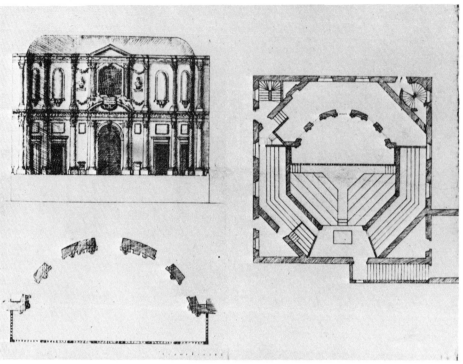

244

245

the several thesis drawings he made from the late 1630s until after the Restoration (e.g. Star Chamber, Barber Surgeon's Theatre, and York Water Gate). However, except for minor details, what this drawing shows is essentially the Cockpit-in-Court as designed by Jones. The drawing is enlightening, revealing the persistence of the Elizabethan form of the playhouse for the production of regular drama. By 1630 (to say nothing of 1660) Jones had brought scenic machinery to a high degree of sophistication; but there is no evidence that the new Cockpit-in-Court had any provision whatever for stage mechanics. Architecturally, the theatre appears to be based on the Teatro Olimpico at Vicenza, not as built, with deep perspectives by Scamozzi, but as designed, before 1580, by Palladio. Jones's stage, with its perspectives and machines, was a stage not for drama but for the masque. A few drawings record occasional adaptations of the masque stage to the production of plays; but only one design reveals that even the Cockpit-in-Court could be transformed to a simple illusionistic theatre if necessary. (J.H. & S.O.)

Wenceslaus Hollar (1607–1677)
245 OLD ST PAUL'S CATHEDRAL FROM THE EAST, AFTER RESTORATION
Engraving
Photograph

Wenceslaus Hollar (1607–1677)
246 DETAIL OF SOUTH SIDE OF OLD ST PAUL'S CATHEDRAL, SHOWING INIGO JONES'S RESTORATION OF THE NAVE
Engraving
Photograph

247 ST PAUL'S CATHEDRAL, *c.*1621
Elevation of west front
Pen, wash and pencil: 46 × 50
Royal Institute of British Architects

248 ST PAUL'S CATHEDRAL, *c.*1636
Elevation of north transept front
Pencil and pen: 59·6 × 44·5
The Provost and Fellows of Worcester College

249 ST PAUL'S CATHEDRAL
Design for the doors on the north and south sides of the nave
Dated: 1637
Pen and pencil: 38 × 27
Royal Institute of British Architects

250 ST PAUL'S CATHEDRAL, WEST FRONT
Engraving of measured drawing by Henry Flitcroft (1697–1769)
Photograph

The seventeenth-century history of St Paul's Cathedral, before its destruction in the Great Fire, is concerned with the embarrassing economic problem of its restoration. A commission was set up in 1608 by James I. Cecil was a member, and Jones's design for completing the tower and spire which had been destroyed by lightning in 1561 was accepted. Stylistically Jones's solution was a mirror image of his design for the New

247

Exchange (28). Jones's famous design for the west front, hitherto associated with the 1631 commission, has now been relegated to 1608. This cannot be. Jones's designs of 1608 are painterly whereas this design is executed in an aggressive manner, which can be ascribed to the experience of Jones's Italian journey in 1614. In fact there is a closer resemblance to drawings about 1620, the paired order against a rusticated face, and the cherub's heads with garlands in the frieze, relate it to the Banqueting House, as does the drafting style of the west door to the *greate Doure* (213) of the Banqueting House dated 1619. If drawings were produced for the Commission of 1620, this must be one of them. Jones was a prominent member of this commission, subscriptions were solicited, and huge quantities of Portland stone acquired. There was certainly serious-ness of intent. The situation changed when William Laud became Bishop in 1625. Before he was translated to Canterbury in 1633, a successful new commission had been set up in 1631 and Jones was ordered to carefully restore the Gothic east parts and choir, and to completely encase the Romanesque nave and transepts in a classical skin.

On January 16th, 1633, the King ordered work to begin at the east end and to progress along the south side to the west. The first accounts date from April 1633, when Edward Kinsman was appointed principal mason. John Webb, who was Clerk Engrosser, seems to have had the administrative control of the building site. The foundation stone of the great west portico was laid in July 1635, and in 1640 the old medieval west gable was taken down and rebuilt, also the north transept was rebuilt. Works stopped in 1642. Sir John Summerson has percipiently shown how Jones reacted to the primitive

252

character of the Norman walls he was encasing; that this was no haphazard application
of a classically ornamented skin, but a profound learned exposition, where each part of
the cathedral was seen to be expressed in an architectonic mood, Tuscan for the nave,
Doric for the aisles and doorways there, Ionic for the portals in the transepts, and
culminating in Corinthian for the tremendous portico. As this portico was the King's
personal offering, Jones saw that this royal gesture was magnificently commemorated
in one of the greatest porticos north of the Alps. It stood 56 feet high, which is only 18
inches lower than the Pantheon. Its direct classical prototype was Palladio's reconstruction of the Temple of Antoninus and Faustina in Rome. In 1636 when this portico
was rising, Jones had been consulted for the rebuilding of the Temple Bar. His proposed solution was no less monumental, a great secular Roman entrance to Fleet
Street, that would lead to the triumph of Caroline Laudianism expressed in stone.
(J.H.)

After Sir Anthony Van Dyck (1599–1641)

251 WILLIAM LAUD, ARCHBISHOP OF CANTERBURY
Oil on canvas: 123·3 × 91·5
The National Portrait Gallery (171)

252 TEMPLE BAR
Design based on Arch of Constantine, Rome
Pen, pencil and wash: 33 × 31
Royal Institute of British Architects

John Webb (1611–1672)

253 TEMPLE BAR, 1636
Pen and pencil: 48 × 35·5
Royal Institute of British Architects

254 TEMPLE BAR
Section of arch of no.253 and an equestrian portrait of Charles I
Inscribed: *Inigo Jones, 1638*
Pen, pencil and wash: 39 × 32
Royal Institute of British Architects

Jones was first asked by the City Council to confer about a new Temple Bar in 1636. The potential symbolic relationship between this secular monument of the City's commercial power, and St Paul's great portico, the gift of the King to the City's House of God, could hardly have been ignored. It would be unwise to suggest that Jones saw Fleet Street as a triumphal way, but it surely did not escape him, that on the King's entry into the City, a royal way would lead to where the Bishop of London and the Lord Mayor waited to receive their monarch, beneath one of the most magnificent porticos in the world. Jones's project for an equestrian statue of the King relates to Le Sueur's statue now at Charing Cross and to Van Dyck's portraits of Charles on horseback. All symbolise Stuart aspirations to Imperial grandeur. (J.H.)

255 WEST FACE OF WINCHESTER CATHEDRAL SCREEN
Pencil and grey wash: 30·5 × 39
Royal Institute of British Architects

Charles Woodfield

256 WINCHESTER CATHEDRAL SCREEN, 1714
Photograph

257 WINCHESTER CATHEDRAL SCREEN
Photograph

Le Sueur (*fl.*1610–1643)

258 JAMES I
Photograph

Le Sueur (*fl.*1610–1643)

259 CHARLES I
Photograph

It is not clear if Jones was involved in the programme of works at the cathedral being carried out around 1636. The central tower was being vaulted 1633–1634, and although the vault matches Bishop Fox's wooden choir vault of *c.*1500, a Latin inscription on the new vault is so arranged to form the Latin numeral for 1635, a conceit that might be thought Jonesian. King Charles had visited Winchester in this year, and his dislike for the ancient pulpitum led to his act of royal piety, in paying for the new screen. The contract between the King and Le Sueur for the two statues in the aedicules was dated June 17th, 1638, and witnessed by Jones. The sculptor was paid a total of £380 and the statues were probably in position by about 1640. Jones's design is made up of elements which figured in his 1620 design for the west front of St Paul's and from the seventh book of Serlio. The screen was dismantled in 1845 and subse-

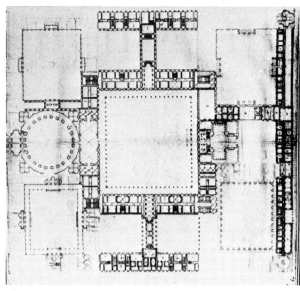

256   260

quently, the centre bay found its way to the Museum of Archaeology at Cambridge. Le Sueur's statues are still in the cathedral. (J.H.)

260 WHITEHALL PALACE

Preliminary study for the P scheme plan for a palace in St James's Park
Pen and pencil: 37·4 × 33·9   Whinney, pl.XI, (b)
Trustees of the Chatsworth Settlement

261 WHITEHALL PALACE

Elevations for river and park fronts of the P scheme
Pen: 40·7 × 67·1   Whinney, pl.XIII, (a)
The Provost and Fellows of Worcester College

262 WHITEHALL PALACE

Elevations of centre block and angle pavilions and other ornamental details of the river front, P scheme
Pen and pencil: 30·1 × 39·3   Whinney, pl.IX
The Trustees of the Chatsworth Settlement

263 WHITEHALL PALACE

Design for the chapel, and ? Council Chamber
Pen and pencil: 33·2 × 21·7   Whinney, pl.XIII, (c)
The Trustees of the Chatsworth Settlement

John Webb (1611–1672)

264 WHITEHALL PALACE

Bird's eye view perspective of K scheme by Webb of *c.*1647, conveying an idea of the three-dimensional mass of the palace. This scheme for the Whitehall site proposed to incorporate and duplicate the Banqueting House.
Engraving, 1749
Photograph

145

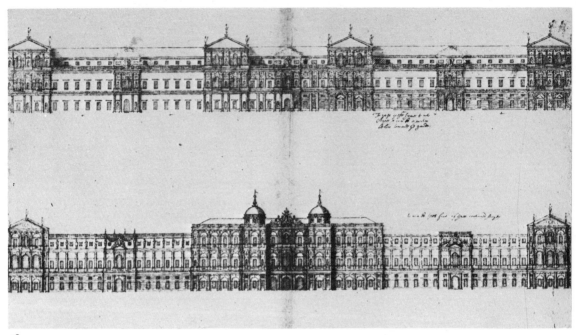

261

The earliest mention of a proposed palace occurs in 1638, when it was rumoured that 'His Majesty hath a desire to build new again in a more uniform sort'. This is also the year of the project for the grand front of Somerset House on the Strand. Jones is not associated with a new Whitehall Palace until 1658, when Sir William Sanderson recalled the late 1630s when a palace in St James's Park was to have been built 'according to a Model drawn by Inigo Jones'. Let it at once be said that not a single drawing or even sketch survives in Jones's hand. All the drawings are by John Webb. Subsequent to the early eighteenth century, all the drawings were attributed indiscriminately to Jones. When William Kent published a group in his *Designs of Inigo Jones* in 1727, neither he nor Lord Burlington understood how to differentiate between styles of draughtsmanship. When J. Alfred Gotch wrote his standard life of Jones two hundred years later in 1928, he dismissed Jones's responsibility altogether. In 1946, Dr Margaret Whinney re-examined the drawings and classified them broadly into two groups comprising seven schemes. She concluded that only four of these could be dated before Jones's death, and they were lettered P, K and C (*c.*1637–9) and T (1647–8). Sir John Summerson examined the drawings anew in 1966 and concluded that of all the schemes, only one can be considered to reflect Jones's style for palace architecture. This is the P or preliminary scheme. It is, incidentally, not for rebuilding Whitehall Palace, but for a site in St James's Park. The P scheme then is the only one from which to truly evaluate the greatest might-have-been in English architecture. It has to be judged against palaces of the day, and these were few. Indeed, there is only the Louvre, incomplete in 1638, and the Escorial, which Jones would have known from engraved views. In garnering his ideas, Jones was a reactionary, drawing upon the eternal classical sources in Antiquity and the Renaissance; Pliny's description of Laurentium, Villalpando's reconstruction of the Temple of Solomon at Jerusalem, the Vitruvian house drawn by Palladio in Barbaro's 1584 edition of Vitruvius,

265

a Roman patrician house from Scamozzi, and also from Scamozzi, the great circular atrium in his reconstruction of Pliny's villa at Laurentium. His elevational and ornamental treatment is also Scamozzian. Indeed, the central block on the river front is based upon a design, that Jones had in his collection, by Scamozzi for a Venetian municipal palace. The big question mark of English architectural history and of Jonesian studies is whether Lord Arundel really possessed 'two chests with architectural designs by Vicenzo Scamozzi', as listed in his inventory in 1655. If he did, and if he had acquired them in 1615, Scamozzi might well emerge as a far more fundamental and formative influence upon Jones, who like Scamozzi eschewed Palladio's more mannerist style. There is, of course, much else in the make-up of Whitehall: a contribution from France in the guise of Lescot's Louvre elevations; something from the many Roman palaces that Jones must have seen; elements from Bolognese late sixteenth century architecture. The result is harmonious and understated. The visual experience of walking through the courtyards, examining the Great Hall, Council Chamber and Chapel, would have been profoundly of antique senatorial Rome. Whitehall could have been a Palace of the ancients. Neither the Escurial, nor the Louvre had this to offer. If we must underline one failure, it is Jones's inability or disinclination to integrate his masses. Like Sir William Chambers, in the following century, he was the master of the small scale unit of design, and Whitehall is a grouping of perfect small units, each an utterly exquisite statement. It is doubtful if it would have looked good today and a gigantic Somerset House is perhaps a valid comparison. It is a design that needed sun to shadow it, to bring it to life. The gloom, mists and soot of London would have soon rendered it an unmoving mass, and it would have been filled with civil servants. (J.H.)

265 HYDE PARK LODGE
Villa elevation
Pen and pencil: 31·5 × 46·5
Royal Institution of British Architects

Although this seminal design has been published as a project for the Queen's House
c.1616, its grammar is very different from the signed and dated 1616 elevation for an
unidentified country house (192) and from other designs ascribed to the Arundelian
period of Jones's career. For this reason a later date is almost certainly probable.
Bagshot Lodge (1631–3) was thought possible, but as Sir John Summerson has
pointed out, it had a portico of four timber columns with stone bases. He suggests,
however, that the Hyde Park Lodge is a plausible candidate. It was built *c*.1634–5
and the accounts for that year (PRO E 351/3268) present a picture of a loggia with
four composite columns and two pilasters at first floor level. The Lodge was of two
storeys, brick, perhaps stuccoed, and had a roof with six dormers. This design was
found among those by Palladio, where it had been since before 1720, when Lord
Burlington acquired the collection. It was he who commissioned Henry Flitcroft to
redraw this design, believing it to be one by Palladio. In the redrawing, Flitcroft
produced an eighteenth century Neo-palladian villa model, the genesis of which can,
in this one respect, be traced back directly to this seminal design by Jones. (J.H.)

Jones and Henrietta Maria

The Architecture

The suite of state rooms at Wilton House, even if they are by Webb, are a unique
survival of the Court style of Jones. Wilton is the only measure by which to recon-
struct a picture of the many interior decorative programmes carried out for Queen
Henrietta Maria. Nearly all Jones's efforts, during this phase of the Surveyorship,
were directed towards the interior improvement of the Queen's palaces. One would
wish that something more had survived to counter the inbalance of Wilton to match
against accounts and designs. More than anything in the Queen's reign, excepting
perhaps the Whitehall Cockpit, a peep at the Somerset House chapel, or the 'new'
Cabinet Room there would have been the most rewarding of experiences. How one
longs to have joined that party, led by Sir William Chambers, through the shut-up
apartments of the old palace, before he demolished them in 1776. The description of
that tour, through faded dusty splendour, is more evocative than any drawing or
itemised account. Work at Somerset House was almost continuous from 1627 to 1637,
and within this decade the Queen was also completing the Queen's House at Greenwich as a country residence. In comparison, work at Oatlands Palace in 1627 and
1635 was of minor consequence, although from 1639 when the King purchased
Wimbledon Palace for the Queen, the extent of alterations there suggests that her
affections had been transferred to this beautiful old country house of the Cecils. At
Wimbledon a Frenchman, André Mollet, was laying out the gardens. He was of the
Queen's entourage and it was natural that she should employ her own countrymen.
The work performed by Jones for the Queen is probably only partly itemised in the

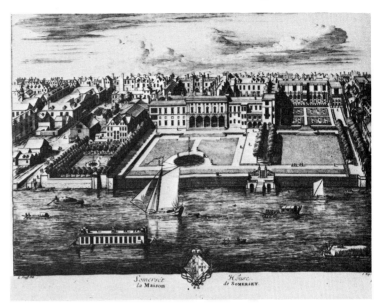

266   267

Declared Accounts, for undoubtedly much was paid for out of her Privy Purse. Although Jones received a pension of £20 a year from Michaelmas 1631 as 'Surveyor of Her Majesty's Works', the Queen privately employed her own French designers, and Jones was obliged to execute, with modifications, their designs. This is the case both at Somerset House and the Queen's House. The name of this designer, principally of chimney pieces, remains unknown, but his contribution adds to the already decisive French flavour of Jones's interiors in the 1630s. (J.H.)

Artist Unknown and Hendrik Van Steenwyck

266 HENRIETTA MARIA, *c.*1635(?)
Oil on canvas: 215·8 × 135·3
The National Portrait Gallery (1247)

The canvas is typical of a series of the King, Queen and courtiers, in which the sitter is placed either within an ideal, but totally imaginary perspective architectural setting, or within a perspective view, drawing the eye in, to contemplate an actual room or vista. Mytens' portraits of the Earl (180) and Countess of Arundel, 1618 are early examples of the latter, in which the viewer's eye is led to consider Jones's picture and sculpture gallery in Arundel House. The former type found its exponent in van Steenwyck, who painted classical architectural backgrounds into which portrait figures were inserted. A number exist of Charles I and Henrietta Maria (e.g. Dresden, Copenhagen and Turin). (R.S.)

267 VIEW OF SOMERSET HOUSE FROM THE RIVER
Drawn by L. Knyff, engraved by J. Kip for *Britannia Illustrata*, 1707
Royal Institute of British Architects

268 THE CHAPEL, SOMERSET HOUSE
Plan from an eighteenth-century survey
Photograph

271

275

Henry Flitcroft (1697–1769)

269 THE CHAPEL, SOMERSET HOUSE
Plan of the ceiling
Pen and wash: 35 × 55
Royal Institute of British Architects

270 THE CHAPEL AT SOMERSET HOUSE, SHOWING THE ALTAR
North (ritual east) elevation
Engraving: Isaac Ware, *Designs of Inigo Jones and Others*, c.1735
Photograph

271 THE ROYAL CLOSET, SOMERSET HOUSE
South elevation
Engraving: Isaac Ware, *Designs of Inigo Jones and Others*, c.1735

272 NICHE OUTSIDE THE CHAPEL, SOMERSET HOUSE
Pen and pencil: 190 × 120
Royal Institute of British Architects

273 NICHE OUTSIDE THE CHAPEL, SOMERSET HOUSE
Pen and pencil: 270 × 200
Royal Institute of British Architects

274 NICHE OUTSIDE THE CHAPEL, SOMERSET HOUSE
Pen and pencil: 26·5 × 18
Royal Institute of British Architects

277   278

275 WINDOW AT THE CHAPEL, SOMERSET HOUSE
Dated: 1632
Pen and pencil: 28 × 45
Royal Institute of British Architects

276 CHIMNEY PIECE IN THE CROSS GALLERY, SOMERSET HOUSE
Design for the installation of a chimney piece in 1636, incorporating parts of an older chimney piece of *c*.1610–1611
Pen and pencil: 40 × 32
Royal Institute of British Architects

Unidentified French Architect
277 CHIMNEY PIECE
Pen and wash: 34·5 × 20
Royal Institute of British Architects

Inigo Jones after a French Architect
278 CHIMNEY PIECE
Dated: *1636*
Pen and wash: 30 × 19
Royal Institute of British Architects

279 THE DOORCASE IN THE NEW CABINET ROOM, SOMERSET HOUSE
Pen and pencil: 32 × 36
Royal Institute of British Architects

280

John Webb (1611–1672) after Inigo Jones
280 WATER STAIRS, SOMERSET HOUSE
Pen and pencil: 41 × 28·5
Royal Institute of British Architects

John Webb (1611–1672) after Inigo Jones
281 THE 'FIRST' DESIGN FOR REBUILDING THE STRAND FRONT OF SOMERSET HOUSE
Dated: *1638*
Pen and wash: 46·4 × 66·7
The Provost and Fellows of Worcester College

John Webb (1611–1672) after Inigo Jones
282 THE 'SECOND' DESIGN FOR REBUILDING THE STRAND FRONT OF SOMERSET HOUSE
Dated: 1638
Pen and wash: 36·2 × 46·4
The Provost and Fellows of Worcester College

In the spring of 1617, Queen Anne of Denmark took up residence in old Somerset House, the Tudor palace of the Protector Somerset. She had but a short time to live and Jones designed only a lantern over the hall. Following her death, Denmark House as it had been re-named, was granted to Prince Charles, who seems to have been disinterested in the palace, and when King, he in turn granted it to his Queen in 1625. Her works, which commenced in 1626, first included a Cabinet Room over the south end of the Privy Gallery, which as Kip shows, had a balcony or pergula (267) directly aligned upon the Water Gate. This Cabinet Room is not to be confused with the New Cabinet Room begun in 1628 (279), which was refashioned from an earlier room at the east end of the Cross Gallery designed in 1610. It too was given an iron balustraded

281

balcony for the view over the river. The accounts convey a picture of a richly painted, marbled and gilded room, of white, gold and blue colours, ornamented with grotesque work. For all this only an exquisitely elegant drawing of the doorway survives. At the other end of the palace, behind a sixteenth-century gabled elevation, was the old tennis court facing the stables. It was replaced from 1630 by the Chapel, whose cruciform plan can be seen in Kip's view, aligned north to south. It was complete in 1635, much damaged during The Interregnum, restored in 1660, and reluctantly demolished by Sir William Chambers in 1775. Survey plans show that this chapel was a double cube of 30 by 30 by 60 feet, with shallow transepts, a vestry behind the altar at the north end, and the Royal Closet at the south end. The exterior had what is described in the accounts as 'three great frontispieces', which may have been pediments in the north and south gables and one on the west transept. It had eight 'great windows of Portland stone', which were distributed, two in the Royal Closet, four in the Chapel proper, and two in the vestry. The west transept, unlike the east, was free of exterior obstruction, and may have had one of the niches (272–273) designed by Jones in its elevation. The accounts and engravings build up a picture of a most sumptuous interior, which must have been one of Jones's most important works. De Critz painted the Closet with grotesque work on a white ceiling, a gilded and walnut coloured entablature, and a frieze with panels of grotesque work containing badges. The capitals were gilded and the windows were white. The screen to the Closet was French in style, taking up motifs that had appeared in Oberon's Palace in 1611, and in the Park Stairs to Whitehall Palace, built in 1624 and remodelled in 1628. The Queen's nationality and the pronounced French influence can hardly be a coincidence and there is evidence that the Queen was employing an anonymous French designer, who is known to have supplied Jones with at least four designs for chimney pieces for here and at the Queen's House, including one inscribed by Jones 'from ye French ambasator'. From this group of designs and this phase of Jones's career, stem the francophile influences that later found expression in the interiors at Wilton House. It is not known if this Frenchman was resident in London and paid for out of the Queen's Privy Purse, or sent his designs from Paris via 'ye French ambasator'.

A substantial interior reconstruction of the 1610 Cross Gallery followed in 1635–

283

1636 (P.R.O., E 351/3269), which included removing Maximilian Colt's chimney piece and giving it a new overmantel, but retaining the waisted pilasters of the fireplace. Work on Somerset House was concluded in 1638, when the Queen's New Closet at the south end of the chapel was fitted up, but for this no designs survive. The imminent conclusion of these interior works may have prompted Jones to examine the problem of the Protector's Strand front, isolated from the rest of the irregular frontage between The Strand and Duchy Lanes. It was the same problem that was to daunt Sir William Chambers in the next century. Jones's solution was to ignore privately owned land and to build a monumental front along The Strand, demolishing the Protector's front, but tying in the central unit with the Tudor courtyard behind. If the Whitehall designs (260–64) were later, then this ambitious project dated 1638 could be regarded as a trial run for them. Jones is here handling a 480 feet front, using a very different type of treatment to Isaac de Caus's proposed front of 400 feet at Wilton House, an almost contemporary project. The principal source for the central block elevations is a project by Scamozzi for a civic building in Venice, a design that is now in the Devonshire Collections at Chatsworth, and must once have been owned by Inigo. The intervening elevations of the larger mezzanined 'not taken' project (281) are partly based upon an elevation in the seventh book of Serlio. Ashton Court in Somerset, built *c.*1628, is perhaps the earliest building in England derived from this Serlian source. (J.H.)

287

Adriaen Van Stalbemt (1580–1662) and Jan Van Belcamp (d.1653)
283 A VIEW OF GREENWICH WITH THE QUEEN'S HOUSE, *c.*1632
Oil on canvas: 81·9 × 106·6
Her Majesty The Queen

The view is from the hill on which the Observatory now stands, overlooking Greenwich Palace and the River Thames. The rambling Tudor palace runs along the riverbank, but in the near distance there is the ground floor of the half-completed Queen's House spanning the road outside the wall of the park. On the hill stand Charles I and Henrietta Maria with the young Prince Charles. The extrovert courtier on the left is Endymion Porter and the figure in black in the foreground right is Richard Weston, 1st Earl of Portland, Lord High Treasurer. (R.S.)

284 THE QUEEN'S HOUSE
Design for the side elevations, with projecting pedimented porticos
Photograph (see 171)

John Webb (1611–1672) after Inigo Jones
285 THE QUEEN'S HOUSE
Plan, with a full portico on one front
Photograph

286 THE SOUTH ELEVATION OF THE QUEEN'S HOUSE
Engraving: Colin Campbell, *Vitruvius Britannicus*, 1715
Photograph

287 THE NORTH ELEVATION OF THE QUEEN'S HOUSE, *c.*1640
Drawing
Photograph

292

Anonymous French Architect, perhaps the Master of French Chimney Pieces
288 CHIMNEY PIECE FOR THE NORTH-EAST CABINET ROOM, THE QUEEN'S HOUSE
Pen and wash: 37·5 × 25
Royal Institute of British Architects

Inigo Jones, after anonymous French Architect
289 THE CABINET ROOM CHIMNEY PIECE, THE QUEEN'S HOUSE
Inscribed and dated by Jones 1637
Pen and wash: 30·5 × 18·5
Royal Institute of British Architects

290 THE NORTH-WEST CABINET ROOM CHIMNEY PIECE, THE QUEEN'S HOUSE
Dated: 1637
Pen and wash: 21 × 20
Royal Institute of British Architects

291 TWO DESIGNS FOR THE BEDCHAMBER CHIMNEY PIECE, THE QUEEN'S HOUSE
Pen and wash: 18·5 × 22
Royal Institute of British Architects

292 A CHIMNEY PIECE AND OVERMANTEL, THE QUEEN'S HOUSE, AND FREELY DRAWN STUDIES
OF PUTTI
Pen and wash: 19 × 29
Royal Institute of British Architects

Anonymous French Architect, perhaps the Master of the French Chimney Pieces
293 A FOUNTAIN AT GREENWICH
Inscribed and dated by Webb: *1637*
Pen and wash: 39·4 × 26
The Provost and Fellows of Worcester College

293

294

John Webb (1611–1672) after an anonymous French architect

294 A FOUNTAIN AT GREENWICH

Pen: 40·7 × 26

The Provost and Fellows of Worcester College

The Queen's House has often been extolled as one of the first purely Italianate buildings in England and therefore of seminal importance, but when Queen Anne died in 1619 work had already been stopped for a year. The H-shaped plan had been fixed but the walls had only risen to the height of the rusticated ground storey. In this sorry state it remained for over twenty years. The question that haunts architectural historians is to know what was first proposed and begun and how this differed to what was finally built after 1630. It cannot be answered, but it is significant that the only documents of pre-1630 source add up to a building of different elevational treatment. It seems impossible to believe that Jones would have carried out to the letter designs made right at the beginning of his career in the Surveyorship.

The earliest surviving drawing of the north front may not be a design, but rather a measured elevation intended to give directions to an Italian painter of trompe-l'oeil decoration, for there are pencilled directions as to *Trofei, Sacrificio*, etc., whilst the central arched window has suggestions for flanking paired caryatids. What is most striking is the odd rhythm of the fenestration, quite different from the 'Georgian' equilibrium of the openings today. The upper windows of the outer bays are grouped by an iron pergula, and the windows below them are shorter by two layers of rustication than those flanking the entrance. The open ground to the north of the Queen's house was probably used for entertainments, which would have been viewed from the upper floor balconies or pergulas.

Similarly, it does not seem possible that Jones would have carried out designs for the

295   296

interior executed before 1618. The surviving designs for chimney pieces date from 1637 and there is no proof one way or the other that they were executed, although presumably chimney pieces of this francophile sort were. The ceiling of the Queen's Bedroom painted by either Matthew Gooderick or John de Critz I, is a rich survival of the gorgeous canopied decoration that such rooms received. Its grotesque antique roman style of ornament can only today be matched by the ceiling of the Single Cube Room at Wilton House. The circular staircase is one of Jones's most beautiful creations, with its elegant ironwork so different to the heavy balustraded stairs that Jones would have seen in such palaces as Caprarola. (J.H.)

295 A CHIMNEY PIECE AT OATLANDS PALACE
Dated: *1636*
Pen and pencil: 29 × 19
Royal Institute of British Architects

296 STUDY FOR THE PAINTING ON THE GARDEN WALL, OATLANDS PALACE
Inscribed: '*for the painting in oyle of the open wale with landscipes in the garden at Oatlandes 1637 to bee a landscip only and no compartment*'
Pen and wash: 16·5 × 25·5
Ashmolean Museum, Oxford

Although parts of the Elizabethan palace have been excavated, the plan of the Carolean accommodation in the palace is still unknown, but it may have been adjacent to the Vineyard. Henrietta Maria does not appear to have used Oatlands for more than occasional visits. This chimney piece (295) is almost certainly the one painted 1636–1637 by Matthew Goodrick 'in a white marble cullor' with 'some parts of the members thereof' gilded for her 'New Cabinet Roome'. If the garden wall *trompe-l'oeil* was also carried out, Goodrick may have painted this too, although it is not clear what sort of landscapes were to be enclosed by the decorative panels. (J.H.)

297 FRIEZES IN THE ENTABLATURE OF A ROOM, WIMBLEDON PALACE
Pen and pencil: 15·5 × 27
Royal Institute of British Architects

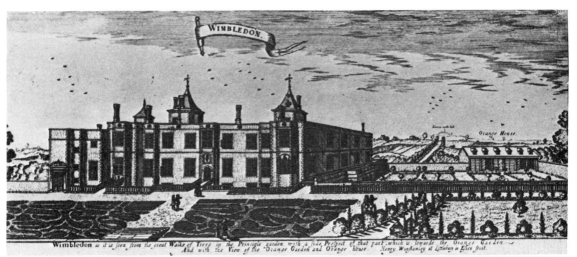

WIMBLEDON

Wimbledon as it is seen from the great Walke of Trees in the Principle garden with a side Prospect of that part which is towards the Orange Garden And with the View of the Orange Garden and Orange house. Henry Winstanley at Littleton in Essex fecit.

Henry Winstanley (1644–1703)

298 WIMBLEDON PALACE, SHOWING THE MAIN GARDEN FRONT, AND SUNKEN ORANGE GARDEN
Engraving: 1678
Photograph

Wimbledon had been built for Sir Thomas Cecil in 1588 and was purchased by King Charles for Henrietta Maria in 1639, the last substantial accommodation acquisition of the Crown. Early in that year 124,000 bricks were made 'for the Queen majesty's work' and by July 1641, Nicholas Stone was supplying chimney pieces; Jones had been paid £558 10s 11d 'for building and repairing at our house at Wimbledon', when André Mollet was laying out the gardens. Jones's work probably included considerable internal alterations, the general re-planning of the west wing, which was given a cruciform plan, and the addition of some external features such as a segmental pedimented door in the west wing and the doorway in the centre of the garden front. (J.H.)

The Plays

Though King Charles took an ardent interest in plays, in fact he dictated to James Shirley and Lodowick Carlell, the plots of *The Gamester* and *The Passionate Lovers*, and rescued Davenant's *The Wits* from the censor's ban, Jones's most important dramas were produced for Queen Henrietta Maria. She commissioned three pastorals, and in the first two, she herself played the lead. *Artenice* (299), by the Sieur de Racan, had been performed at the French court in 1619, and Henrietta Maria commanded a production *à la française* to entertain the King in the first year of his reign. *Artenice* is a landmark in British theatrical history, the first regular drama to be presented on a perspective stage with moveable scenery. Four productions for a royal visit to Oxford in 1605 must be discounted, as these were imitations of ancient plays, and Jones's stage was essentially archaeological, based on suggestions in Vitruvius and his Italian Renaissance interpreters. However in 1616, Jones's settings changed seven times, and his scenic devices included thunder and lightning, the rising of the moon, and a view of Somerset House and the Thames. The Queen's participation was considered suffici-

299

ently scandalous to cause severe embarrassment to the King; no lady had ever taken a speaking part on the British stage before. It was not until 1633 that such a production was undertaken again; this time it was an English pastoral by Walter Montagu. *The Shepherd's Paradise* (301–303) was ostensibly designed to give the Queen practice in speaking English, but it was also heavily burdened with Neo-platonic philosophy, and took almost eight hours to perform. The audience was, not surprisingly, unenthusiastic.

A few weeks later William Prynne, Puritan and barrister of Lincoln's Inn, spoke for a large body of outraged public opinion when he included in his virulent attack on the stage, *Histrio-Mastix, or the Scourge of Players*, the famous index entry 'Women-Actors, notorious whores'. Though Prynne insisted that no slur was intended on the Queen, he was indicted for high treason, convicted and sentenced to life imprisonment, fined £5,000, disbarred, deprived of his academic degree, and his ears were cut off by the public executioner. The court took its theatre seriously.

The last of the Queen's pastorals was the anonymous French play *Florimène* (304, 305), performed by her maids of honour in 1635. The victory over Prynne had been won, but Henrietta Maria was in the last month of pregnancy, and was content to be a spectator. (s.o.)

Honorat de Bueil, Sieur de Racan, *Artenice*, February 21st, 1626

299 PROSCENIUM AND STANDING SCENE
Pen and brown ink, washed with grey, squared with lead for enlargement: 34·4 × 45
O&S 135; S&B 67
The Trustees of the Chatsworth Settlement

The play was performed as privately as possible, because of the controversial appearance, not only of women on the stage as actors, but of the Queen herself. Both Florentine and Venetian correspondents described it as beautiful, but Chamberlain captures

300

the mood of contemporary court and town gossip: 'I have knowne the time when this wold have seemed a straunge sight to see a Quene act in a play but *tempora mutantur et nos*'. Jones's design shows the standing scene, one based directly on Serlio's famous wood engraving of the *Satyric scene*. The annotated copy of the play, in the Houghton Library at Harvard University, contains further information about scene changes, which included the moon in the night sky, a wood and a pastoral village, closing with a view of Somerset House and the Thames. (R.S.)

Unknown Play at Somerset House, 1629–30

300 ?THE TRAGIC SCENE
Pen and brown ink washed with brown, and squared with a point for enlargement: 31·2 × 40 o&s 141; s&b 365
The Trustees of the Chatsworth Settlement

On December 8th, 1629, a warrant was issued to Jones 'for a Stage and Scene to be made at Somerset House'. The identification of the Tragic Scene, as the stage erected on that occasion, is no more than a tentative one. As in the case of the set for Racan's *Artenice*, also for Somerset House and closest to it in style, there are no side pilasters to the proscenium arch. Above, there is a crown adorned with *fleurs de lys* appropriate to Henrietta Maria, flanked by Hercules and Truth. Stylistically the drawing cannot be later than 1630. The basis of the setting is Serlio's famous wood engraving of *The Tragic Scene*. (R.S.)

301

Walter Montague, *The Shepherd's Paradise*, January 9th, 1633, probably repeated on February 2nd.

301 PROSCENIUM AND STANDING SCENE
Pen and black ink squared with a point for enlargement: 20·1 × 26
O&S 245; S&B 69
The Trustees of the Chatsworth Settlement

302 ACT V: LOVE'S CABINET
Inscribed below: *Loves Cabinett of Relieve*
Pen and brown ink, squared with black lead for enlargement and splashed with green and brown scene-painters' distemper: 27·3 × 29 O&S 250; S&B 167
The Trustees of the Chatsworth Settlement

303 BELLESA, ALIAS SAPHIRA, PRINCESS OF NAVARRE
Inscribed at top: *Belleza; the cronet of perle/not so bige/ The lase on sleve and/brest not so bigge.*
Pen and black and brown ink: 23·9 × 15·4 O&S 255; S&B 168
The Trustees of the Chatsworth Settlement

The Shepherd's Paradise was one of the Queen's Neo-platonic pastorals, acted by her and her ladies, and lasting no less than seven or eight hours. As in the case of other plays, as against masques, designed by Jones they were never conceived as requiring specific settings, and Jones always has to invent a repertory of appropriate backgrounds. B.M. Stow MS 976 contains annotations listing some of the scenes which included a 'pallas scene through trees', 'the Temple', 'a woode', and 'the Tombe'. This drawing is typical of Jones's style in the mid to late thirties, with the use of pen without wash and heavy shading in the foreground. (R.S.)

302

303

Florimène, December 21st, 1635

304 PROSCENIUM AND STANDING SCENE

Pen and brown ink: 29·7 × 35·3 L&S 326; S&B 243

The Trustees of the Chatsworth Settlement

305 ACT V, SCENE I: THE SECOND TEMPLE OF DIANA

Brown ink, squared with black lead for enlargement: 24·6 × 37·5 O&S 333; S&B 251

The Trustees of the Chatsworth Settlement

Florimène was performed in honour of the King's Birthday by a group of French actors in the Hall of the Whitehall Palace. As in the case of *The Shepherd's Paradise*, it was a saga of Neo-platonic love in the manner of Honoré d'Urfé's *Astrée*, enlivened from time to time by *intermedii*, scenes of relieve depicting the seasons. The angled side wings, of trees and cottages, remained in position throughout the play. The ground plans and elevations (144–151) give us a remarkable insight into the technical side of this production. (R.S.)

304

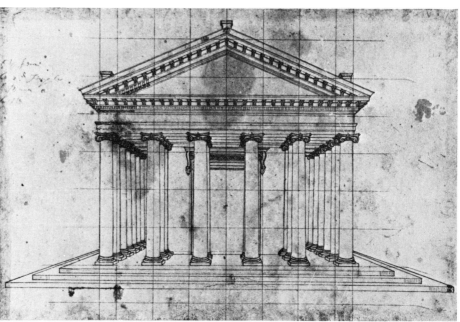

305

The Royal Masques, 1631–40

In a very profound way the theatre was King Charles's truest kingdom. No other English monarch was so intensely concerned with his own image, and in the splendid series of masques that Jones created for him in the 1630s, we may see the royal imagination fashioning through the art of his Master Surveyor as with van Dyck and Rubens, an ideal realm and an ideal self. In part, the King's involvement with these spectacles was a political act: to control the way people saw the monarch was to control their response to the royal policy as well, or that at least was the theory. But in a larger sense, the Caroline masques are not directed at an audience. They are reflecting and perfecting devices, magic mirrors in which Charles saw himself and his rule as he wished them to be. By 1637, when he told his nephew, the Palsgrave, that he considered himself the happiest monarch in Christendom, he had found a way of looking at his world that made him seem so.

To an absolute monarch ruling by Divine Right, the masque is an eminently logical form. It celebrates the power of princes; its spectacular visions of peace and harmony are articles of faith and assertions of divine will. This is how Charles regarded his annual performances; the directness with which Caroline masques served as symbolic justifications of the royal policy, in particular, current issues, can only imply that Jones's chief collaborator, after 1630, was the King himself. Under this lavish patronage, Jones produced his most ambitious artistic achievements, expressions of the royal will and mirrors of the royal mind.

Jones's last works with Ben Jonson were two masques for the season of 1630/31, *Love's Triumph through Callipolis* (306, 307), in which the King danced the lead, and *Chloridia* (309–311), with the Queen at its centre. Jonson's verse is elegant and lyrical, but the lightness of touch is deceptive; for the two works are elaborately Neo-platonic, and philosophically as arcane as anything the poet ever wrote. To modern readers they appear admirably suited to the court's tastes, and indeed they announce the mythology of Charles's reign, with the King appearing as a classical heroic lover, the Queen as a goddess of chaste love. But in fact they were the bitter end of a long and fruitful union. Jones, angered at finding that Jonson's name stood first on the title-pages of the printed texts, terminated the collaboration. For the remainder of his career, Inigo Jones was the 'Inventor' of the Caroline masque.

The next year, 1632, the court again saw a pair of masques. The King's allegory expressed the triumph of power and magnanimity, the Queen's that of beauty and virtue. As the Emperor Albanactus in *Albion's Triumph* (314), Charles was a noble complement to Henrietta Maria as Divine Beauty in *Tempe Restored* (318). Jones's poet was Aurelian Townshend, who was suitably self-effacing.

For the season of 1634 the King suggested that the Inns of Court present him with a masque; the work would serve at once as a display of loyalty and a repudiation of the nefarious Prynne, who was awaiting trial. The Inns lavishly complied; the result was *The Triumph of Peace* (319, 320). James Shirley composed the text in Consultation with a committee of lawyers, and Jones produced the work in the Banqueting House. Its subject was the relation between the King and the law, and it was diplomatically, covertly, but also unqualifiedly critical of certain of the royal policies. This is the only instance we have of Charles's critics retaining Inigo Jones in an attempt to speak to the King in his own language. The attempt was vain, although the masque was a huge success; the royal solipsist saw nothing but adulation in the production, and was graciously pleased to order it repeated.

Two weeks later, the King himself danced in Thomas Carew's great *Coelum Britannicum*, in which the British court becomes a model for Jove's heaven. Apotheosis can go no further, and Jones's superb drawing for the opening scene of the work is a good index to how closely Carew's idealism was in touch with the imagination of both his designer and his King. This work is a brilliant expression of the spirit of the age; and with the possible exception of *Comus*, it is poetically the finest masque in English.

Between 1635 and 1640 Jones produced four masques in collaboration with Sir William Davenant. The year after *Coelum Britannicum* (321–325), the court saw the Queen in *The Temple of Love* (326–328) banish sensuality and licentiousness, in the persons of certain Asian magicians, from the realm. In 1638 Charles as Britanocles, ruler of the ocean, danced the triumph of the ship-money act in *Britannia Triumphans* (329–332), and the Queen, in *Luminalia* (333–335) celebrated the absolute power and virtue of the monarchy in a vision of the purest Platonism. Jones's final production took place in 1640, on the eve of the Civil War. After the triumphs of the decade, *Salmacida Spolia* (336–345) is almost elegiac. The Spoils of Salmacis are the spoils of the King's peace; Charles is Philogenes, lover of his people, a patient, suffering, Christ-like hero. The sainted martyr of *Eikon Basilike*, staging his own masque nine years later, is only a step beyond. (s.o.)

Ben Jonson, *Love's Triumph through Callipolis*, January 9th, 1631

306 ?DRAFT DESIGN FOR SCENE 2: THE SEA TRIUMPH
Pen and brown ink: 18·8 × 23·1 O&S 147; S&B 230
The Trustees of the Chatsworth Settlement

307 A WHINING, BALLADING LOVER
Pen and brown ink, washed with grey: 17·1 × 98 O&S 150; S&B 69
The Trustees of the Chatsworth Settlement

308 A MELANCHOLY DESPAIRING LOVER
Pen and black ink, washed with grey: 18·2 × 11 O&S 158; S&B 77
The Trustees of the Chatsworth Settlement

Love's Triumph and *Chloridia* opened the series of royal masques that span the years of Personal Rule. In them, the roles of Charles and Henrietta Maria are defined and all the masques subsequent to these elaborate the basic statements made by Jonson and Jones in 1631. *Love's Triumph* is a celebration of the ideals of Platonic love and virtue, as expressions of autocratic power, the King arriving as Heroic Love attended by the lords as other forms of exemplary love. This victory is expressed by Jones in his sets, which move from the city of Callipolis, from which the evil forms of sensuality are banished, to a seascape across which the King floats as the embodiment of maritime power (royalist policy foundered on Ship Money), of love sprung, like Venus, from the sea and of reason triumphing over the passions. The masque casts Charles and Henrietta as the Platonic ideals of both intellect and will, virtue and beauty respectively. No opposition is voiced or uncertainty admitted. King and Queen in the masque contemplate further scenic marvels, which emblematically celebrate aspects of their own perfection: a rock arises bearing the muses, who sing of the Renaissance of the arts effected by such rule, and Venus, the celestial embodiment of Platonic Love, descends to contemplate her human counterpart.

306

307

308

309

The relationship of this drawing (306) to *Love's Triumph* is tentative, but it is the only recorded masque with sea mythology which fits. It is a rare instance of Jones sketching a stage peopled with actors and masquers: the latter arrive in a boat to the right, singers probably stand by the side wings to the left; Neptune and a sea deity float at the back, while on the upper stage a celestial tableau is revealed. This may have been inspired by Buontalenti's setting for Arion, the fifth of the 1589 Florentine *intermezzi*.

This is not the only source Jones has drawn upon: The Melancholy Desparing Lover (308) is arranged in the classic pose of a melancholy lover; whereas the Whining Ballading Lover (307) is based on Callot's Bernovalla in the *Balli di Sfessania*. (R.S.)

Ben Jonson, *Chloridia*, February 22nd, 1631

309 SCENE I: A LANDSCAPE
Pen and brown ink squared with a point for enlargement: 39·6 × 49·9
O&S 163; S&B 82
The Trustees of the Chatsworth Settlement

310 CHLORIS: PRELIMINARY SKETCH
Pen and brown ink: 30·2 × 19·8 O&S 178; S&B 95
The Trustees of the Chatsworth Settlement

311 CHLORIS: FINAL DESIGN
Fine pen and brown ink washed with grey: 26·2 × 15 O&S 181; S&B 98
The Trustees of the Chatsworth Settlement

310   311

Chloridia continues the story of *Love's Triumph* (306–308) and is directly complementary to it. In it, the vices of the underworld of the court are anatomised and allegorised in anti-masques of violence, both human and elemental, which are banished from the stage by Juno, goddess of marriage. Once more, there is a celebration of the royal couple and the perfection of their union, the true ends of love, and again Jones expresses it by means of a visual progression through storms and tempest to the rainbow of peace, hovering above the Queen, as Chloris enshrined in the midst of 'a delicious place', a garden in flower, the perfect image of bountiful nature tamed by man. As in *Love's Triumph*, this gives birth to a renaissance of the arts and Fame flutters into the clouds, while below she is surrounded by Poesy, History, Architecture and Sculpture.

Chloridia marks an important stage in the development of Jones's stage mechanics, that is the invention of the fly gallery, which enabled the curtain to rise, the introduction of a storm and the ascent of Fame. The first scene (309) was probably inspired by Giulio Parigi's set for Mount Ida in *Il Giudizio de Paride*, 1608. The costume sketches for Henrietta Maria (310, 311) are an instance of Jones's obsession with the masquers' costumes. In comparison, the designs for the anti-masquers are mechanical, but no less than eight drawings and two alternative designs were made for Henrietta Maria to choose from. Below no. 311 is an interesting note indicating that the design was submitted for the Queen's inspection. Jones offers to change anything, including the colour, although the greens he chooses he considers to be 'most propper'. (R.S.)

312   314

Inigo Jones and Aurelian Townshend, *Albion's Triumph*, January 8th, 1632

312 PROSCENIUM ARCH
Pen and brown ink washed with purplish grey, the shield and putti at the top with green. Squared with a point, black lead and ink, for enlargement, and splashed with reddish brown scene-painters' distemper: 38·2 × 42·4 O&S 190; S&B 107
The Trustees of the Chatsworth Settlement

313 SCENE I: A ROMAN ATRIUM
Pen and brown ink washed with purplish grey and splashed with scene-painters' grey distemper: 37 × 40·2 O&S 191; S&B 108
The Trustees of the Chatsworth Settlement

314 ALBANACTUS: FINAL DESIGN
Pen and grey ink washed with grey: 28·4 × 14·2 O&S 205; S&B 123
The Trustees of the Chatsworth Settlement

From 1632 onwards Jones 'invented' the subject matter of the masques, probably in consultation with the King, and employed a series of poets of varying qualities to give voice to his ideas. *Albion's Triumph* has the most autocratic vision of Charles who is cast as the Roman Emperor Albanactus. A Roman Imperial Triumph is put on the stage and the new visions of the peace and order of Caroline rule are seen by Jones entirely in architectural terms: an atrium, a forum, an amphitheatre, a stately temple and a view of Whitehall Palace. The King is presented flanked by his consuls and attended by priests and sacrificers. Whitehall Palace is placed within an architectural sequence from classical antiquity, and depicted as embodying the abstract principles of Charles's rule: Innocence, Justice, Religion, Affection to the Country and Concord, all com-

315   316

panions of Peace, hover in the clouds above it.

The proscenium arch is an assertion of the status of architecture as a liberal art with the twin figure of *Theory* and *Practice* flanking the arch and it is Jones's reply to Jonson after their final quarrel in 1631. The figures are based on the title page of Serlio (1619).

Scene 1 (313) is based on Giulio Parigi's Temple of Peace in *Il Giudizio di Paride* (1608), the amphitheatre and most of the costumes on Panvinio's book on triumphs (103) and most of the rejected characters on dresses in Vecellio (126, 128, 130). (R.S.)

Inigo Jones and Aurelian Townshend, *Tempe Restored*, February 14th, 1632

315 SCENE I: THE VALE OF TEMPE
Pen and brown ink: 35·6 × 38·6 o&s 216; s&b 139
The Trustees of the Chatsworth Settlement

316 CIRCE
Pen and black ink: 17·2 × 15·6 o&s 219; s&b 141
The Trustees of the Chatsworth Settlement

317 INFLUENCES OF THE STARS
Pen and black ink washed with grey: 26 × 16·7 o&s 239; s&b 156
The Trustees of the Chatsworth Settlement

318 DIVINE BEAUTY AND THE STARS
Pen and brown ink washed with grey: 25·2 × 15 o&s 244; s&b 161
The Trustees of the Chatsworth Settlement

The Queen's masque, *Tempe Restored*, based on Balthasar de Beaujoyeulx's *Balet Comique de la Reine* danced at the French Court in 1581, tells the story of the vanquishing of the evils of the passions (represented by Circe) by the heroic example of the King, the embodiment of rational order and intellect. In it Jones deployed his most spectacular machines to date to place on stage the harmony of the spheres and to achieve the descent of the Queen, playing her celestial counterpart, Divine Beauty, in a chariot of

317

318

gold and jewels. Jones's commentary is outspoken in its belief that man apprehends through images: 'Corporeal beauty', he writes, 'consisting in symmetry, colour and certain inexpressible graces . . . may draw us to the contemplation of the beauty of the soul, unto which it hath analogy'.

Besides scenic marvels, Jones's production was remarkable for the first appearance of professional women singers on the stage. Madame Coniack played Circe (316) and Mistress Shepherd played Harmony. The side wings in Scene 1 (315) were copied from Giulio Parigi's 'The Garden of Calypso' in *Il Giudizio di Paride*, 1608. The design for Henrietta Maria's costume is an instance of Jones providing alternatives; flaps lift revealing variations on head-dress, bodice and skirt. (R.S.)

319

320

James Shirley, *The Triumph of Peace*, February 3rd and February 13th, 1634

319 PROSCENIUM ARCH
Pen and brown ink washed with grey, squared with a point for enlargement, and splashed with grey scene-painters' distemper: 48 × 55·1 O&S 267; S&B 180
Royal Institute of British Architects

320 THE SONS OF PEACE
Pen and brown ink washed with grey. The outline has been traced with a point and the back of the paper rubbed with black lead for enlargement: 30·5 × 92
O&S 274; S&B 190
The Trustees of the Chatsworth Settlement

The Triumph of Peace was demanded by Charles I from the Inns of Court as a peace-offering for William Prynne's implied attack on the Queen's theatricals in his virulent *Histrio-Mastix*. Although produced at the apogee of Charles's Personal Rule, it represents an attempt to speak to him in his own language, and it uses the masque as a vehicle for the bold political statement by the lawyers who organised it, that the Royal Prerogative cannot exist without the aid of Law. The King's Peace and Law are interdependent: 'The world shall give prerogative to neither. We cannot flourish but together'.

The Masquers, as the Sons of Peace (320) were discovered in 'a delicious arbour' and the Queen declared that she 'never saw any masque more Noble'. By royal command it was repeated in Merchant Taylors' Hall on February 13th, bearing witness of the failure of the masque as a form to bear its message to the King. (R.S.)

321

322

323

324

325

Thomas Carew, *Coelum Britannicum*, February 18th, 1634

321 PROSCENIUM AND MOUNTAIN SCENE
Pen and brown ink washed with brown, squared with lead for enlargement and
spattered with blue and green scene-painters' distemper: 39·5 × 30·2
O&S 277; S&B 227
The Trustees of the Chatsworth Settlement

322 ABANDONED PROJECT FOR COELUM BRITANNICUM
Pen and brown ink: 29 × 30·2 O&S 278; S&B 228
The Trustees of the Chatsworth Settlement

323 SCENE I: SIDE WINGS OF A CITY IN RUINS
Pen and brown ink, squared with a point and black lead for enlargement and splashed
with scene-painters' brown distemper: 40·8 × 45·8 O&S 279; S&B 192
The Trustees of the Chatsworth Settlement

324 ATLAS
Pen and black ink washed with grey, squared with a point and black lead for enlarge-
ment and splashed with scene-painters' distemper: 39 × 25 O&S 280; S&B 197
The Trustees of the Chatsworth Settlement

325 SCENE V: A GARDEN AND A PRINCELY VILLA
Pen and brown ink squared up for enlargement and splashed with green scene-
painters' distemper: 43·7 × 56·5 O&S 281; S&B 247
The Trustees of the Chatsworth Settlement

326

Coelum Britannicum is the greatest of Caroline court masques, remarkable for its poetry by Thomas Carew and for its tissue of ideas, interlocked with visual emblems, conjured up by Jones expressing the climax of Stuart autocratic ideals. Carew used Giordano Bruno's dialogue *Lo Spaccia de la Bestia Trionfante* as a basis for creating a spectacle of extraordinary richness and breadth of vision. The plot is that of a reformation of the heavens, the banishment of the wicked vicious Ovidian constellations from the sky to be replaced by the star constellations of the Olympus of the Stuart Court. It opens amidst the classical ruins (323) of a city of the Ancient British and reaches its climax in King, Queen and court contemplating a princely villa with gardens in the new manner (325) as the ideals of a new civilisation. Charles and the lords are British heroes of a new age, that of Great Britain, that mighty union achieved by Stuart rule, and Jones produced his most spectacular machine to give expression to this achievement. A vast hill arose from below stage bearing figures representing England, Ireland and Scotland, above which sat the Genius of Great Britain who later ascended into the fly gallery. As in *Albion's Triumph* the masque closed with the abstract ideals of Charles's rule, Religion, Truth, Wisdom, Concord, Reputation and Government, hovering in the clouds above a royal palace, this time Windsor Castle. This was Jones's supreme achievement of stage mechanics, using no less than three levels of stage simultaneously.

As usual in Jones's designs, the sets are derivative; the proscenium arch and mountain scene (321) is a combination of a border from an engraving of the *Coronation of the Virgin* by Federigo Zuccaro with Giulio Parigi's 'The Fleet of Amerigo Vespucci' in *Il Giudizio di Paride* (1608), the side wings of ruins (323) are adapted from Parigi's Palace of Fame in the same series of *intermezzi* and the princely villa and garden (325) from an engraving by Antonio Tempesta. (R.S.)

327   328

Sir William Davenant, *The Temple of Love*, February 10th, 11th and 12th and possibly 14th, 1635

326 PROSCENIUM
Pen and brown ink washed with warm grey, squared with a point for enlargement: 39·2 × 43 O&S 292; S&B 210
Royal Institute of British Architects

327 SCENE 3: AN INDIAN SHORE
Pen and brown ink, splashed with green and brown scene-painters' distemper: 23·2 × 33·1 O&S 295; S&B 229
The Trustees of the Chatsworth Settlement

328 MAGICIANS, A PRIEST AND A POET
Pen and brown ink: 27·3 × 18·9 O&S 297; S&B 213
The Trustees of the Chatsworth Settlement

The Temple of Love casts Henrietta Maria in her assumed role as the Queen of Love, Indamora, who brings to Britain the new pure Neo-platonic Love. This vision of the Queen and her ladies, as the quintessence of the cult, is prefaced by a defeat of lust, in the figure of certain Asian magicians (328), by Divine Poesy. It ends on the familiar Caroline themes, the exultation of the royal marriage as an ideal pattern and of the King as the embodiment of 'the last and living hero'.

Jones's scenic contribution led the spectators' eyes through the mists obscuring the Temple of Chaste Love to a seascape (327) upon which floated Indamora and her attendant ladies in 'a maritime chariot made of spongy rock stuff mixed with shells, seaweeds, coral, and pearl'. The triumph closed with architecture, the temple of Chaste Love revealed, and the god himself descending.

The design for an Indian shore is based on Giulio Parigi's 'The Fleet of Amerigo Vespucci' in *Il Giudizio di Paride* (1608). Jones's detailed supervision of each part of every costume is caught in the long annotations on the design for the magicians (328).

(R.S.)

329

333

331

332

Sir William Davenant, *Britannia Triumphans*, January 17th, 1638

329 SCENE 1: ENGLISH HOUSES WITH LONDON AND THE THAMES AFAR OFF
Pen and brown ink: 27·2 × 36·2 O&S 334; S&B 258
The Trustees of the Chatsworth Settlement

330 SCENE 2: A HORRID HELL
Pen and brown ink, splashed with brown and pale blue scene-painters' distemper:
30 × 34·7 O&S 336; S&B 193
The Trustees of the Chatsworth Settlement

331 ANTI-MASQUERS
Pen and brown ink: 27·7 × 18·3 O&S 343; S&B 261
The Trustees of the Chatsworth Settlement

332 SCENE 4: THE PALACE OF FAME
Pen and brown ink: 29·2 × 37·3 O&S 339; S&B 300
The Trustees of the Chatsworth Settlement

Britannia Triumphans resumed the masques after a break of two years, the cessation of revels being due to the insertion of Rubens's canvases into the Banqueting House ceiling. By the autumn of 1637 the political situation had changed, and the temporary masquing house Jones erected in two months went up while the famous Ship Money case was being tried in the Courts. The masque, always used by Jones as a means of expressing the King's will, was about Ship Money. Charles was cast as Britanocles, 'the glory of the western world', who had reduced his own and far distant seas to order (by the suppression of piracy which was the official justification for Ship Money) and brought to his land a knowledge of arts and sciences, the result of his imposition of order.

The sets epitomise this increasingly unrealistic view of a disintegrating reality. Jones

179

334

335

opens his masque with a glimpse of the new town architecture with a perspective leading to the restored St Paul's (329). He takes the audience through a hell scene (330)
and a mock romantic forest to a culmination in the architectural glories of the Palace
of Fame (332) and, finally a vision of the achievements of Ship Money, the British fleet
sailing into a haven. (R.S.)

Sir William Davenant, *Luminalia*, February 6th, 1638

333 SCENE I : NIGHT
Pen and brown ink washed with grey: 26·7 × 36·9 O&S 383; S&B 308
The Trustees of the Chatsworth Settlement

334 SCENE 2 : TRANSFORMATION SCENE
Pen and brown ink: 25·2 × 29·3 O&S 385; S&B 385
The Trustees of the Chatsworth Settlement

335 DRAFT SKETCH FOR THE QUEEN'S COSTUME
Pen and brown ink: 29·7 × 17·5 O&S 390; S&B 312
The Trustees of the Chatsworth Settlement

Luminalia was staged almost simultaneously with the pyrrhic victory of the Star
Chamber's judgement in favour of the King that *rex* was *lex*. It used the vehicle of the
journey through a single night (an idea derived from a Florentine entertainment of
1608) through a nocturnal night-scene (333) via a city floating in the clouds on a rainbow (334) with fantastic dream figures to a vision of Henrietta Maria as 'queen of
brightness', ushered in by dawn. Once more the masque was about autocratic power,
this time conceived in its purest terms of light defeating darkness, and once more, this
was linked to the artistic programme of the Caroline court, for this 'goddess of brightness' welcomes the persecuted Muses, fleeing from the mainland of Europe.

336

337

338

340

The scenery again is derivative, the nightscene being based on an engraving by Goudt after Elsheimer (114) and the cloud scene (334) is based on Parigi's *intermezzo* 'The Return of Astraea' in *Il Giudizio di Paride* (1608). (R.S.)

Sir William Davenant, *Salmacida Spolia*, January 21st, 1640, repeated February 16th, 17th and 18th.

336 SCENE 1: A STORM AND A TEMPEST
Pen and brown ink, splashed with pink and dark green scene-painters' distemper: 19·2 × 30·9 O&S 401 ; S&B 323
The Trustees of the Chatsworth Settlement

337 SCENE 2: A PEACEFUL COUNTRY
Pen and brown ink: 29·7 × 41·3 O&S 402; S&B 328
The Trustees of the Chatsworth Settlement

338 SCENE 3: THE WAY TO THE THRONE OF HONOUR
Pen and brown ink, a scale for enlargement on the right hand margin, splashed with green scene-painters' distemper: 20 × 28·9 O&S 404; S&B 339
The Trustees of the Chatsworth Settlement

342

341

339

343

344   345

339 SCENE 3: INTERIOR OF THE GREAT CLOUD
Pen and brown ink (cut out): 17 × 27·5 O&S 408; S&B 350
Photograph

340 SCENE 4: THE SUBURBS OF A GREAT CITY
Pen and brown ink: 31 × 42·3 O&S 409; S&B 355
The Trustees of the Chatsworth Settlement

341 FURIES
Pen and brown ink: 29·5 × 21·6 O&S 416; S&B 324
The Trustees of the Chatsworth Settlement

342 HEADDRESS FOR A FURY
Pen and brown ink: 28 × 18·5 O&S 417; S&B 326
The Trustees of the Chatsworth Settlement

343 ANTI-MASQUERS: TWO GROTESQUES OR DROLLITIES
Pen and brown ink: 31·4 × 19·8 O&S 428; S&B 338
The Trustees of the Chatsworth Settlement

344 SKETCH FOR THE KING'S COSTUME
Pen and brown ink: 29 × 16·8 O&S 432; S&B 341
The Trustees of the Chatsworth Settlement

345 THE QUEEN'S COSTUME
Fine pen and brown ink over grey wash: 26·7 × 16·6 O&S 422; S&B 354
The Trustees of the Chatsworth Settlement

Salmacida Spolia was the last of the Caroline masques, a spectacle in which both King and Queen took part. By the date of its performance the political situation had deteriorated so badly that Charles was forced to convene Parliament. The masque is full of wistful memories of royal power at its apogee, the King's Peace. Charles is still cast as the Divine King, but this time as a monarch doomed to live in adverse times. The image of the King gradually assumes the mask of martyrdom, and on the proscenium arch Innocence and Forgetfulness of Injuries, attributes of Christ, take their place side by side with more familiar virtues.

The masque is overtly political. Jones guides the audience through a tempestuous storm (336), the evils which ferment opposition to the sacrosanct rule of Charles, whose blissful reign is next conjured up in a luscious landscape at harvest time (337). There is something pathetic and moving in the Genius of Great Britain imploring Concord not to forsake her: 'Yet stay! O stay! if but to please the great and wise Philogenes . . .'. Charles as Philogenes, the lover of his people, reveals himself no longer in autocratic triumph but as a remote *idea* of Platonic kingship, glimpsed amidst the fastnesses of rocky inaccessible mountains (338). 'The people's giddy fury' is blamed for this mutation in the true order of things and both king and queen are now less patterns of perfection which, once revealed, are tamely followed by their subjects but self-contained ideals within themselves. Jones's final scene (340) is his last poignant statement of the ideals of the Caroline world, his own ideals, the vision and creation by the Vitruvian architect-engineer of harmony upon earth through the introduction of order to architecture. In this final tableau the spheres actually descend and touch the very tops of the buildings of which on earth they were the reflection (R.S.)

Jones and Civic Architecture

Anonymous

346 COVENT GARDEN PIAZZA, *c.*1649
Oil on canvas: 55·9 × 106·6
Collection of Mr G. H. Marwood

Wenceslaus Hollar (1607–1677)

347 COVENT GARDEN PIAZZA, *c.*1658
Engraving
Photograph

348 COVENT GARDEN PIAZZA
Plan of the piazza, plan, elevation and section of St Paul's, elevation of the arcaded buildings
Engraving: Colin Campbell, *Vitruvius Britannicus*, II, 1717
Photograph

349 TUSCAN GATEWAY, COVENT GARDEN PIAZZA
Demolished
Photograph

346

Jones held a key position as a member of a Commission, which issued a proclamation of May 2nd, 1625, prohibiting new building in London, except rebuilding on old foundations. With this proclamation in mind, Francis, 4th Earl of Bedford obviously took care that he involved Jones in his plans to commercially exploit the ground at old Covent Garden. His success was complete on January 10th, 1631, when the Attorney General ordered the preparation of a licence for the Earl to build 'howses and buildings fitt for the habitacons of Gentlemen and men of ability'. We do not know what the Earl might originally have had in mind for his development, but under Jones he got the first rationally developed area of London, a square in which the church played an important visual and theoretical part. As John Evelyn stated, it is probable that the idea of such a square originally came from Leghorn, which Jones must have seen; but the Place Royale in Paris was also of equally formative influence. Sir John Summerson has shown how Covent Garden is a highly subtle exposition of the Tuscan order, perhaps initiated by the Earl's low church wish for economy and simplicity. It would certainly not have been economic to build and ornament expensively. Walpole's well-known anecdote that in reply to the Earl's wish to have a church not 'much better than a barn', Jones replied that he should have 'the handsomest barn in England', is indicative that Jones saw in this necessary economy a challenge to his inventiveness. For a Protestant church there was no classical precedent in England, but the temple form was the obvious solution, and if it was to be of the simplest form, then Jones had to search for a Tuscan order, and he found this in Barbaro's edition of Vitruvius 1556, which had the added authority of being drawn by Palladio. The appropriateness of Tuscan had long exercised Jones in certain situations; in 1615 he had used Scamozzi's Tuscan for the Newmarket Brew House; in 1620 Jones had reconstructed Stonehenge as a Tuscan Roman temple, and in 1629 the Sculpture Gallery at St James's Palace had been based upon a Tuscan atrium. His triumphant application of this order was here at Covent Garden, and even today after countless restorations the nobility and

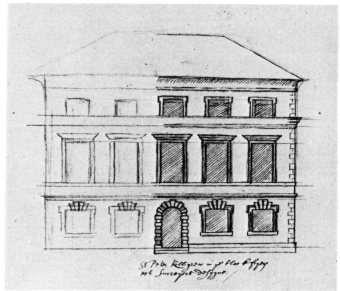

350

351

gravity of his portico is at once apparent. It is no less Neo-classical than any other archaeological reconstruction after 1760, and it would seem that in Europe only Jones could have done this at the time. The Tuscan mood was continued by the two gateways that flanked the church, where the order was a 'lower' rusticated one, and was taken up again in the four blocks of piazza houses that were built on the north and east sides of the square. Here the order is reduced to a stark simplicity. As at Wilton House, Isaac de Caus plays an enigmatic role. He was undoubtedly the Earl's executant architect, as he had been at Woburn Abbey and was probably at Bedford House, the garden of which fronted the south side of the square with a raised terrace and remarkably classical garden buildings. There is, however, no proof that de Caus had any more than executive authority, or any evidence that he tampered with this cerebral exercise in town planning. (J.H.)

John Webb (1611–1672) after Inigo Jones
350 BARBER SURGEON'S ANATOMY THEATRE
Dated by Webb: *1636*
Pen: 47·5 × 35·5
The Provost and Fellows of Worcester College

The first mention of a proposed anatomy theatre for the Barber Surgeons Company, adjacent to their Hall in Monkwell Street, is recorded in the Company's Minutes on February 11th, 1636. In May, it was written that Jones was to provide designs and it was to be 'ovally built' and linked to the Hall by an open gallery or balustraded arcade. At the end of July 1637, work was nearly complete and the domed ceiling was painted with the constellations and planets. The Theatre was so admired by Lord Burlington, that he paid for its repair in 1730; following this he almost certainly initiated its engraving for Isaac Ware's *Designs of Inigo Jones and Others*. Horace Walpole thought it Jones's finest work. Ware's engravings and Webb's drawing do not agree in particulars. Ware, however, must show what existed as he was then Burlington's assistant and

186

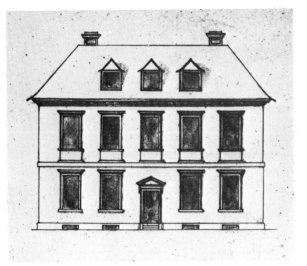

352   353

may have been concerned in the restoration. Webb's drawing is probably on a more ideal plane. The Theatre was demolished in 1784. (J.H.)

John Webb (1611–1672) after Inigo Jones

351 SIR PETER KILLEGREW'S HOUSE IN BLACKFRIARS, LONDON
Inscribed by Webb: *Mr Surveyors desygne*
Pen and pencil: 20·4 × 30·5
The Provost and Fellows of Worcester College

This may not have been built, but for the late 1620s, which is the probable date of this drawing, it is a unique example in England of a rendition of an Italian palazzo-style house. This design was achieved, however, through the experience gained from the Prince's Lodging at Newmarket and Fulke Greville's house, both before 1620. (J.H.)

Lord Maltravers's Development in Lothbury, London.

352 AN ASTYLAR HOUSE
Inscribed and dated by Jones: *Lothbury, 1638*
Pen and wash: 40 × 31
The Provost and Fellows of Worcester College

353 A DESIGN FOR A HOUSE WITH A BALUSTRADED PLATFORM AND A HEXASTYLE PORTICO
Pen and pencil: 22·3 × 26·7
The Provost and Fellows of Worcester College

354 AN ASTYLAR TERRACE WITH TWO ENTRANCES
Pen: 31 × 39·3
The Provost and Fellows of Worcester College

John Webb (1611–1672) after Inigo Jones

355 A UNIFIED GROUP OF SHOPS
Pen and wash: 32·4 × 42
The Provost and Fellows of Worcester College

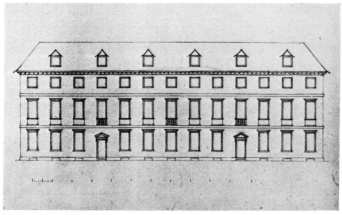

354

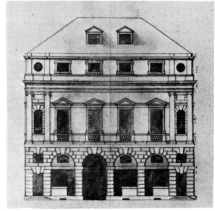

355

Lord Maltravers was the eldest son of the Earl of Arundel. He established at Lothbury an office and manufactory for the minting of royal farthing tokens. It is not certain that all these designs are related, although the house with the balustrated platform (353) is, in fact, the same size as the more simple 1638 design (352), which in turn is related to the thirteen bay terrace (354). All likewise resemble parts of the Covent Garden development (346–349), in particular the three bay houses that flanked the church. If the terrace was built, it was the first regular astylar front in London. Campbell could not improve upon it, when he built his group of houses in Old Burlington Street. Indeed so dependent were his houses upon this Lothbury design, that he might have seen it in 1720. Although the design for a unified group of shops is drawn by Webb, it must be a design by Jones, and the mid 1630s a probable date. (J.H.)

Jones and Country Houses

For one who initiated in designs so many prototypes for English country houses it is odd that no single country house can be proved by documents to have been designed by him. Jones as the country house designer is a mythological figure. He was clearly unwilling to be drawn into the country house round of designing. Courtiers' architecture between about 1620 and 1650 is almost entirely of a mixed classical style, that is usually associated with the names of Nicholas Stone, Balthasar Gerbier, or the, as yet unevaluated, and probably under-valued, Edward Carter. The east front of York House (Gerbier, 1628), Long Ashton (Unknown, c.1628), Cornbury (Stone, 1632), Kirby Hall (Stone, 1638+), or Tart Hall (Stone, 1638), all typify a style of composition that is diametrically opposed to the pure architecture of Jones's royal works. There is a very relevant comparison to Wren's Surveyorship, 1670 to 1700, but whereas Wren was able to delegate commissions to Hawksmoor and Talman, knowing that they were as able as he, Jones had no such subordinates. Indeed, from his Olympian heights, he must have derided the faulty grammatical structure of so many courtiers' houses. The exception is still Raynham, which is an astonishing cross-fertilization from Jones's designs. Its east front centre, the first temple feature in English architecture, was

356

designed after 1622, it would have been extraordinary even ten years later. Chevening can only be dated between 1616 and 1630. Its plan was not Jonesian and its elevation, although innovating, may owe something to Genoese palaces and to Edward Carter. Stoke Bruerne is perhaps the most Italianate house ascribed to Jones. It is, in fact, too Italianate and its pavilions could sit happily in some Roman garden. Wilton, on the other hand, is a design composed of Italian and French influences. There is probably some truth in this, for Wilton is not composed in a very Jonesian way and if Jones really master-minded it, then he seems to have left its execution in the hands, first of Isaac de Caus and then, after the fire of 1647–1648, in those of John Webb. To Webb must go the credit for designing the state rooms, a precious reminder of Jones's royal style in the franco-phile manner for Queen Henrietta Maria's works. (J.H.)

356 RAYNHAM HALL, NORFOLK, FROM THE SOUTH WEST
Photograph

Sir Roger Townshend was learned in architecture. He built his house empirically and slowly, so although it was begun as early as 1622, the elevations may not have been decided in detail before the mid or late 1620s. However, Raynham is still a unique surviving Jonesian work of the time and a wonderful synopsis of designs by Jones, especially those for Newmarket. It may not be unconnected that Newmarket Palace was on Sir Roger's road to London, and he could not have failed to stop there to see the Prince's Lodging. Although so many of its parts are purely Jonesian, lack of cohesion in composition proclaims Raynham the work of an amateur, but this does not lessen the impact of the splendid east front centre, the first temple feature in any English country house. (J.H.)

357

357 CHEVENING, KENT, FROM AN ESTATE MAP, 1679
Photograph

358 CHEVENING, KENT, PLAN AND ELEVATION
Engraving, Colin Campbell, *Vitruvius Britannicus*, 1717
Photograph

Chevening was inherited by the 13th Lord Dacre in 1616 and tradition states that
Jones designed the house before Dacre's death in 1630. Even if it is nearer 1630 than
1616 it is nevertheless a revolutionary statement. There are allusions in its elevational
designs to the later designs for Sir Peter Killegrew (351) and Lord Maltravers (352–
355), as well as to earlier designs such as the one at Chatsworth (189) for Fulke
Greville. However, it is also Genoese, and may therefore be by Edward Carter who had
made designs for Easthampstead *c.*1630 upon a Genoese plan from Rubens' *Palazzi
di Genova*, 1622.

Anonymous

359 SIR FRANCIS CRANE, *c.*1625–30
Black and red chalk: 17·8 × 14
The British Museum

360 STOKE BRUERNE, PLAN AND ELEVATION
Engraving, Colin Campbell, *Vitruvius Britannicus*, 1725
Photograph

361 STOKE BRUERNE, PORTICO OF THE WEST PAVILION
Photograph

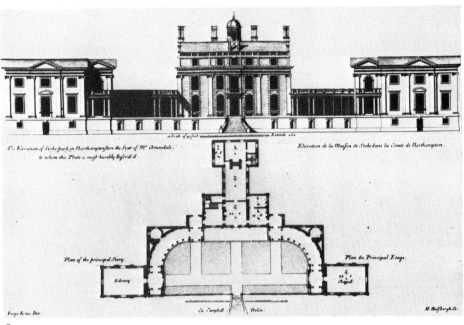

360

362 STOKE BRUERNE, WEST PAVILION FROM THE EAST
Photograph

Sir Francis Crane was one of the new ambitious men of the Caroline court and had been secretary to Charles, when Prince of Wales. In 1619 he had built a house at Mortlake to house his tapestry works. Stoke Bruerne was granted to him in 1629 and building there may have ceased in 1635, when Crane had to retire to France for his health. The pavilions and colonnades are a coherent design and are derived from Italian sources, such as the quadrants from Palladio's Villa Meledo, and the juxtaposition of giant and secondary orders from Michelangelo's Capitoline. In fact so Italianate are these pavilions, that Crane, as tradition states, brought the design out of Italy. These are certainly more Italianate than any other design by Jones, who never borrowed an element so literally in this way. Crane was a highly cultured man and could well have acted for Stoke Bruerne as Townshend did for Raynham (356). Coherence disappears with the main block. It seems to have had shaped gables to the roof ends, of a type that is found on some late sixteenth-century Northamptonshire manor houses. Indeed, perhaps its esoteric plan was a re-working of an older house on the site. The elevation is a *mêlée* of influences in stark contrast to the clarity of the pavilions. Its date is uncertain, but there is no doubt that Jones had nothing to do with it, even if it has a grant order. (J.H.)

Isaac de Caus (?–*c*.1656)
363 WILTON HOUSE, SOUTH FRONT AND PARTERRE
Prospect drawing for engraving
Pencil and pen: 45 × 58·5
The Provost and Fellows of Worcester College

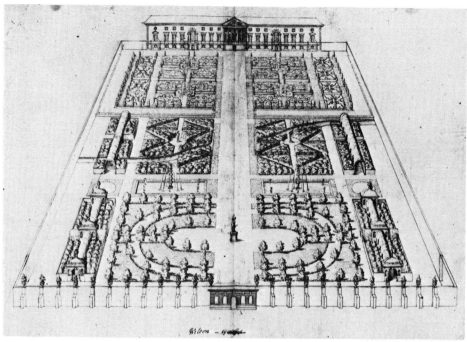

363

364

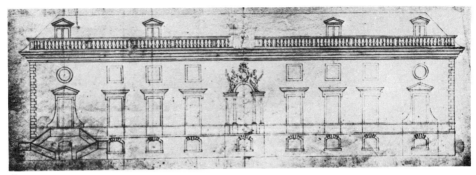

365

366

367

Isaac de Caus(?–*c*.1656)

364 WILTON HOUSE, SOUTH FRONT AND PARTERRE
Engraved in *Le jardin de Vuillton*
Pencil and pen: 43·2 × 55·9
The Provost and Fellows of Worcester College

Isaac de Caus (?–*c*.1656)

365 WILTON HOUSE, REDUCED VERSION OF THE SOUTH FRONT
Pencil and pen: 15·5 × 44·5
Royal Institute of British Architects

366 WILTON HOUSE, CEILING FOR THE COUNTESS OF PEMBROKE'S BEDCHAMBER
Pen and wash: 35·5 × 48
The Provost and Fellows of Worcester College

367 WILTON HOUSE, CEILING FOR THE COUNTESS OF CARNARVON'S BEDCHAMBER
Pen and wash: 36·2 × 48·3
The Provost and Fellows of Worcester College

371

372

368 WILTON HOUSE, PASSAGE ROOM INTO THE GARDEN
Pen and wash: 35·5 × 48
The Provost and Fellows of Worcester College

369 WILTON HOUSE, CEILING OF THE CABINET ROOM
Pen and wash: 35·5 × 48
The Provost and Fellows of Worcester College

John Webb (1611–1672)
370 WILTON HOUSE, CABINET ROOM
Pen and wash: 35 × 27·5
Royal Institute of British Architects

John Webb (1611–1672)
371 WILTON HOUSE, PANELLING
Pen and pencil: 29·2 × 33
The Victoria and Albert Museum

John Webb (1611–1672)
372 WILTON HOUSE, PANELLING
Pen and pencil: 29·6 × 36·2
The Victoria and Albert Museum

373 WILTON HOUSE, PLAN OF STATE ROOMS AND NORTH WING
as replanned after the fire in 1707.
Engraving, Colin Campbell, *Vitruvius Britannicus*, 1717
Photograph

Isaac de Caus (?–c.1656) and Inigo Jones
374 WILTON HOUSE, SOUTH FRONT
Photograph

Isaac de Caus (?–c.1656)
375 WILTON HOUSE, THE HUNTING ROOM
Photograph

374

375

377

John Webb (1611–1672)
376 WILTON HOUSE, SINGLE CUBE ROOM
Photograph

John Webb (1611–1672)
377 WILTON HOUSE, DOUBLE CUBE ROOM
Photograph

Wilton is the *locus classicus* of the English Palladian house, yet the serenity and visual perfection of its great south front is certainly the result of compromise. Jones played a very curious, negative part in its story, for all the designs as executed are by de Caus and Webb. Whatever 'advice and approbation' (John Aubrey's words) Jones may have given, the great porticoed design for a front of 400 feet, twice as long as built, is clumsy and ineffectual as a composition. It bears no comparison, if judged by the same standards, to the Somerset House elevation of 1638. The decision to restrict the front to a rebuilding on the foundations of the old house, which had two Tudor towers, may have been taken before the pedimented design was seriously contemplated. De Caus's design for a shorter front could have been built, but if it was, the evidence was destroyed in the fire of 1647–1648. On the other hand, the front today with the pavilion towers *al italiano*, to use Aubrey's words again, could be a rebuilding with some modifications of the pre-fire front. Jones's advice may well have been given to solve a problem perhaps beyond de Caus's abilities; to reduce a large design to a smaller one and come out with a satisfactory solution. The key, however, must always have been the positioning of the Tudor towers. It would almost seem an act of serendipidy that one of the most beautiful elevations in English architecture should be the result of compromise

379   380

and many minds. The state rooms are all post-fire and there is no reason to deny Webb the credit for them, although the plan must have been determined before the fire. Perhaps the series of ceiling designs made by Jones and now in Worcester College were executed in the house before the fire. It might be supposed that an apartment for the Countess of Carnarvon would have been provided after the Earl's death in 1643. All the other drawings point to Webb's responsibility for the decoration of the Double Cube, Single Cube and other south front rooms. The decorative painting was executed by Edward Pierce, who was responsible for scenery for the court masques and thus provides us with the only reminder of the quality of scene painting demanded by Jones. To John Webb must go our thanks for providing the only surviving memorial of a suite of rooms, resembling those royal apartments decorated by the Surveyor. Their ambience makes us regret what has been lost. (J.H.)

Gateways

378 IONIC GATEWAY WITH A BROKEN SEGMENTAL PEDIMENT
Pen, pencil and wash: 44·5 × 34·5
Royal Institute of British Architects

379 GATEWAY WITH A BARRED OVAL OPENING IN THE PEDIMENTED PANEL
Pen and wash: 41 × 30
Royal Institute of British Architects

380 GATEWAY ON THE KING'S ROAD AT BEAUFORT HOUSE, CHELSEA, FOR THE EARL OF MIDDLESEX, 1621
Pen and wash: 41·5 × 26
Royal Institute of British Architects

381

387

381 THE BEAUFORT HOUSE GATEWAY NOW AT CHISWICK HOUSE, MIDDLESEX
Photograph

382 GATEWAY AT NEW HALL, ESSEX, FOR THE MARQUIS OF BUCKINGHAM IN 1623
Pen and wash: $35 \times 30\cdot5$
Royal Institute of British Architects

383 GATEWAY AT NEW HALL, ESSEX
Pen and wash: 36×27
Royal Institute of British Architects

384 GATEWAY AT HATTON HOUSE, ELY PLACE, LONDON, FOR THE DUKE OF LENNOX,
1622–1623
Pen, pencil and wash: 36×29
Royal Institute of British Architects

385 GATEWAY FOR HATTON HOUSE, ELY PLACE, LONDON, FOR THE DUKE OF LENNOX,
1622–1623
Pen and wash: 44×28

382

383

384

385

386

388

386 GATEWAY INTO THE PARK AT ST JAMES'S PALACE, 1627
Pen and wash: 37 × 25
Royal Institute of British Architects

387 TUSCAN GATEWAY, NOW DEMOLISHED, FORMERLY FLANKING ST PAUL'S CHURCH, COVENT GARDEN, *c.*1632
Photograph

388 GARDEN GATEWAY, LITTLE HADHAM, HERTFORDSHIRE
Artist: Cornelius Johnson, 'Arthur Capel and his Family', *c.*1639
Photograph

Anonymous, seventeenth century
389 GARDEN GATEWAY
Watercolour: 15 × 20
Royal Institute of British Architects

Jones was perennially fascinated by the variety of architectural display possible in gateways. This variety is shown in his surviving designs, but there were many more gateways, at least two at Greenwich, five at Oatlands, one or more at Whitehall. They would often be used as vehicles for the exposition of the orders of architecture. The two gateways flanking St Paul's Covent Garden (387) were, appropriately, of the Tuscan order, and so was the St James's Gate (386), and another built there in 1631, which followed the Tuscan theme of the colonnaded open-air sculpture gallery built in 1629. Lord Capel's garden at Little Hadham (388) is a perfect Jonesian layout with antique statues and fountains, a classical gazebo, and like Oatlands, with a 'gateway into ye parke'. Jones's sources for these gates are nearly always Serlio, Vignola or Francart, which he re-adjusts and refines. The Beaufort House Gateway (381) is a direct borrowing from one by Vignola at the Villa Lante. (J.H.)

Jones's Legacy

Architecture

If the term 'Court style' is used to describe Jones's work for King James and King Charles, then it is descriptive of a style of Palladianism that was generally not appreciated by courtiers. Because Jones's subordinates, such as Nicholas Stone or Edward Carter, did not understand the grammar of his style, their buildings are often artisan and impure. They may have vigour and individuality, but they were far from the Jonesian ideal. The great Buckingham epitomises just how insensible a courtier in the King's inner cabal could be to Jones's Palladianism. There is no doubt that his Second Lodging in Whitehall, a building commissioned in 1619 as a royal tribute, was Jonesian. Designed by Jones, its Dining Room had the beautiful coffered ceiling for which the design survives at Worcester College (217). In 1623 Buckingham employed Jones at New Hall for minor interior works and for typical Jonesian garden gateways, but when he wished to build a classical front to York House in 1628, he was content for Sir Balthasar Gerbier to produce a poor reflection of Jones's disciplined style, to be seen not far away at the Banqueting House. For its date, York House was a creditable effort, but it was nonetheless artisan, with typical motifs such as oval windows.

Ashton Court in Somerset, built for Sir John Smyth about 1628, displayed similar characteristics. Again it has ovals and also a monotonous array of closely spaced, but otherwise classical windows. Two other houses typify the mixed style of courtiers; Nicholas Stone's additions to Kirby Hall, Northamptonshire, carried out for Sir Christopher Hatton III from about 1638; and the mysterious unidentified house in the background of Wenceslaus Hollar's engraving of Spring, dated 1643. Both houses possess shaped pedimented gables and pergulars above doorways, the leit-motifs of the Arundellian phase of Jones's style. Also, they have oval or circular windows, which are basically Serlian in derivation, and appear for the first recorded time in a classical context at Sir John Danver's house at Chelsea, possibly as early as 1622. In the variety of fenestration and grouping of horizontal layers of windows irregularly with vertical grouping, the Hollar house seems to be related in some way to Elias Holl's work in Augsburg. Apart from a common usage of motifs, it is clear that there is no relationship between the building style of the courtiers, except for a shared inability to understand the grammar of classical architecture. There are, of course, exceptions that demand investigation. Typical is the screen at Castle Ashby, a work for the Earl of Northampton, *c.*1635, which is as Jonesian in character as a work by another architect could be. Yet it is not even by Webb.

John Webb was the lone inheritor of Jones's court style, and through him the Jonesian ideal of a country house style was promulgated. In 1638, Webb was 27 years of age, and the annotated and worked-over designs for Hale Park of that year, may be his first commission without Jones's superintendence. Not surprisingly, it conforms to the Jones canon, a miniature version of the Hyde Park Lodge or even the Bagshot Lodge. During the next twenty years he produced a succession of majestic designs for country houses or palaces, that carried the Jonesian torch through the dark days of the Interregnum. The Duke of Lennox's Cobham design of 1648 (395), the Countess of Rutland's Belvoir of 1654 (396), John Maynard's Gunnersbury of 1658 (397), and following the Restoration, in 1661, Queen Henrietta Maria's New Gallery at Somerset

390

392

House (398) and the Duke of Somerset's Amesbury (399, 400), all proclaim their indebtedness to models and ideas initiated by Jones. (J.H.)

Jacob Esselens

390 YORK HOUSE, WESTMINSTER
Detail from drawing in the National Library, Vienna
Photograph

This shows an addition between the river front and the sixteenth-century chapel. It may be the room designed by Sir Balthasar Gerbier *c.*1627–28. Although Esselens' view is not to be trusted in minute details; artisan mannerisms are the oval windows, the rather odd articulation of the main cornice and the attic storey, and the use of an elongated full giant order, framing the central bay with a balcony as at the later Nun Appleton in Yorkshire. The mason here was almost certainly Nicholas Stone, who executed the Duke's Water Gate. (J.H.)

391 ASHTON COURT, SOMERSET, SOUTH FRONT
Photograph

Sir Thomas Smyth of Ashton refers to his new building in 1629, so it must have been designed 1628 at the latest. Although the variety of windows, their spacing, and use of irregularly spaced ovals combined together are bad grammar, Ashton is one of the most remarkable non-Jonesian façades of the decade. The basic source is Serlio's seventh book, which is a section of his compendius work that provided both Jones and his subordinates with an inexhaustible quarry of ideas. A comparison between Ashton and Jones's design for the Strand front of Somerset House of 1638 (281–82), which draws upon the same source, is instructive of the gap between the King's style and that of his courtiers. (J.H.)

391

Wenceslaus Hollar (1607–1677)

392 UNIDENTIFIED HOUSE, appearing in *Spring*, 1643
Engraving
Photograph

Hollar was extensively patronised by Lord Arundel. He drew, for example, Arundel House and his country seats at Albury and Arundel Castle. The most likely candidate for this important 'artisan' house is Tart Hall, designed for the Countess of Arundel by Nicholas Stone from 1638. It stood on the corner of Buckingham Gate. However, what Hollar's engraving shows does not fit in with other fragmentary descriptions of Tart Hall. Nevertheless, there is a very clear relationship between the fenestration of this house and Stone's Goldsmiths' Hall of 1634. With its balconied central window, the Serlian tripartite grouping of oval and circular windows, and pedimented gables, the secondary sources for the house are all to be found in the Arundel phase of Jones's Italianism. It is also indebted to another and far more interesting source, the buildings of Elias Holl in Augsburg. In the variety and layered arrangement of windows, there is a distinct relationship to the Augsburg Town Hall. Not only was this engraved, but drawings of it are in the Jones–Webb collection at Worcester College. (J.H.)

393

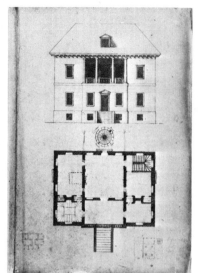

394

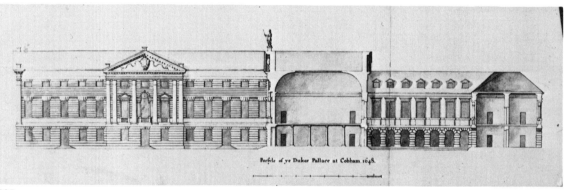

Porfyle of ye Dukes Pallace at Cobham. 1648.

395

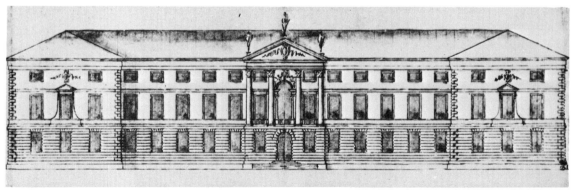

396

393 KIRBY HALL, NORTHAMPTONSHIRE, NORTH FRONT FROM THE FORECOURT
Photograph

Sir Christopher Hatton III, that 'generall sercher of all antiquityes concerning the whole Kingdome', employed Nicholas Stone to design and build huge extensions to an already vast house. Here again are all the familiar artisan details, ill-mannered but nevertheless impressive. Kirby shows, more than any other house, Stone's inability to control and proportion an elevation with regular fenestration. Kirby's attraction lies in its non-conformity (by default of knowing) and robustness. (J.H.)

394 HALE PARK, HAMPSHIRE: LODGE IN THE PARK
Photograph

This design was made for John Penruddock in 1638. It was probably Webb's first work carried out independently of Jones, for three sheets of drawings show him working out the problems of design. There is an obvious relationship to the Hyde Park and Bagshot Lodges, and the Queen's House, which all share the common feature of a portico *in antis*. (J.H.)

395 COBHAM HALL, KENT, DESIGN FOR REBUILDING THE ELIZABETHAN HOUSE, 1648
Pen and watercolour: 41 × 92
The Provost and Fellows of Worcester College

This project, commissioned by James, 4th Duke of Richmond and Lennox, proposes a complete Palladian encasing of the old Late Elizabethan house, which had been completed in the 1590s. Here, Webb can be seen breaking away from the style of his master, to create his own, which is demonstrably more Baroque. (J.H.)

396 BELVOIR CASTLE, RUTLAND, DESIGN FOR A NEW HOUSE
Pen and wash: 18 × 38
Royal Institute of British Architects

The 8th Earl of Rutland preferred Haddon Hall in Derbyshire. It was his Countess who persuaded him to commission designs for rebuilding the castle at Belvoir, which had been slighted in the Civil War. Webb was attending there in July 1654 and these designs belong to this period. Although they were unexecuted, Webb was probably responsible for the later rebuilding of the castle to its old plan from 1662. Tribute must be paid to Newmarket and Whitehall in the composition of this design. (J.H.)

397 GUNNERSBURY HOUSE, MIDDLESEX, PORTICOED ENTRANCE FRONT
Engraving, Colin Campbell, *Vitruvius Britannicus* I, 1715
Photograph

A brick and stone-detailed house, this represents in many ways the quintessence of a Jonesian house, drawing upon Newmarket and the Queen's House for inspiration. It was built for John Maynard from 1657–58. (J.H.)

The Elevation of GUNNERSBURY neer BRANTFORD in the County of MIDDLESEX by Inigo Jones.

Elevation de La Maison de GUNNERSBURY aux Demes Lieue du BRANTFORD dans la Comtè de MIDLESEX

397

Extends 151
a Scale of 60 Feet
The Elevation of the Great Gallery in SOMERSET House to the River
Is most humbly Inscribed to His Grace the Duke of Montross principal Secretary of State &c.

Elevation de La grande Gallerie Del Hostel de SOMERSET du coste de la Riviere est tres humblement Dedie aMonsigneur le Duc de Montross &c.

398

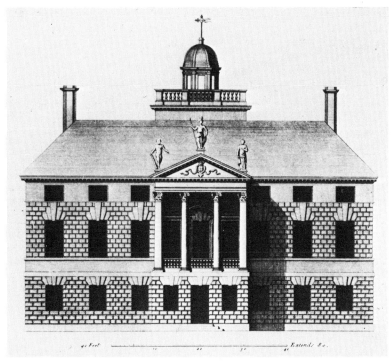

399

398 THE NEW GALLERY AT SOMERSET HOUSE
Engraving, Colin Campbell, *Vitruvius Britannicus*, I, 1715
Photograph

This Gallery comprised the rebuilding of the wing of Somerset House facing the river between the Privy Gallery and the Chapel. This was carried out in 1662 for Henrietta Maria, the Queen Mother. On the basis of a sketch for a pilastered elevation over an arcaded ground floor, drawn by Webb on one of the Whitehall designs, this New Gallery has frequently been attributed to Jones as a posthumous design. This is highly unlikely, but in any case a common source, available to Webb in engravings would have been sixteenth-century palazzi in Bologna, especially those by Tibaldi. (J.H.)

Wyatt Papworth (1822–1894)
399 AMESBURY ABBEY, WILTSHIRE, MEASURED DRAWING OF THE ENTRANCE FRONT
Photograph

Wyatt Papworth (1822–1894)
400 AMESBURY ABBEY, WILTSHIRE, MEASURED SECTION SHOWING CENTRAL SALOON
Photograph

Amesbury, built for the Marquis of Hertford, in 1661, represents Webb's triumph in country house design and the apogée of his style. In C. R. Cockerell's words, its 'uncommon grandeur' 'fills and occupies the mind' and 'for economy of convenience with proportion & effect, it may challenge any Ho: in England ancient or modern'. Amesbury was rebuilt by Thomas Hopper in 1834. (J.H.)

Theatre

Fifteen years elapse before scenery of the type evolved by Jones for the masques makes a cautious reappearance. The masque scenery with its potent images of royal power was anathema to the opposition. Milton in his discussion of William Marshall's famous frontispiece to the *Eikon Basilike*, in which Charles I is depicted as the suffering Christ-king surrounded by emblems of his martyrdom and beatification, scorns it as a 'masking scene . . . set there to catch fools and silly gazers'. 'But quaint emblems and devices', argued Milton 'begged from the old pageantry of some Twelfth Night's entertainment at Whitehall, will do but ill to make a saint or martyr'. With the last of the masques in 1640, stage scenery as moving Neo-platonic tableaux comes to an end.

The transmission of the art of scenic spectacle to the Restoration theatre we owe to John Webb, who had worked with Jones on the later masques. In 1656 William Davenant presented privately, at Rutland House, an opera entitled *The Siege of Rhodes*, with Webb providing the settings. After the Restoration, this was transferred to the public stage and scenery became the norm in the public theatre. (R.S.)

William Davenant, *The Siege of Rhodes*

John Webb (1611–1672)

401 PROSCENIUM AND STANDING WINGS
Pen and brown ink: 22·3 × 36·6   Festival Designs, 107
The Trustees of the Chatsworth Settlement

The Siege of Rhodes was presented privately in Davenant's house. The space in which Webb had to present his spectacle was diminutive; the room was 11 feet high, the stage 18 feet wide and a little over 18 feet deep. The side wings indicated here stayed in position throughout the performance. This was not unusual. Jones had used the same system in *Florimène* (144–51, 304–5). The same designs were almost certainly used when Davenant re-staged the play in 1663 in a public theatre, the Duke of York's, Lincoln's Inn Fields. On to the public stage he ushers the Jonesian tradition of providing scenery invented for the play 'as an accompaniment to the exposition of the plot used in a sort of counterpoint' (Southern). As in the case of Jones's design for Caroline court plays, the settings do not back a scene of action with relevant scenery or change in direct relation to the action before it. At no point does the scenery present a precise location directly related to the spoken dialogue. (R.S.)

John Webb (1611–1672)

402 SECTION OF THE STAGE for *The Siege of Rhodes*
Drawing, British Museum, Lansdowne MS.1171
Photograph

403 DIAGRAM OF THE SECTION OF THE STAGE for *The Siege of Rhodes*
Photograph

Webb's stage technique is directly adapted from Jones's in the final masque, *Salmacida Spolia* (152–57, 336–45), although space forbade the introduction of the normal upper stage. Three sets of side wings and cloud borders, which remained stationary throughout the play, were backed by a series of back shutters, behind them the normal area for scenes of relieve and, finally, the back cloth. This system, in which scenery moved in grooves, was to become the norm in the English theatre into the nineteenth century. (R.S.)

The Surveyor's Last Years, 1640–1652

Very little is known of Inigo Jones in his last years. When Civil War broke out in 1642, Jones was already nearly seventy, a considerable age for the seventeenth century. In July of that year he was in attendance on the King at Beverley, when he lent him the sum of £500. Three years later he was taken prisoner at the storming of Basing House. The house itself was a battered ruin, the furnishings sacked, even the guttering and roof taken away. Jones was ignominiously stripped by the soldiery and carried away in a blanket. The news-sheets on Basing refer to Jones as 'the King's Surveyor, and Contriver of Scenes for the Queen's Dancing Barne'. His estate was sequestered, but eventually restored in July 1646 on the payment by Jones of £545 and a further £500.

Darkness then enfolds the last years and the only fact we know is his death in Somerset House on June 21st, 1651. He died a wealthy man, his legacies totalled £4,150, £2,000 of which went to his relation Anne, wife of John Webb, and a £1,000 to her five children. A £100 was set aside for a monument of white marble in St Benet's, the Jones family church. A drawing by John Aubrey (405) records its appearance shortly after the Great Fire: a sarcophagus tomb with a bust of Jones flanked by obelisks (emblems of eternity) with *bas reliefs* at each end, one depicting the Whitehall Banqueting House, the other, the west porch of St Paul's Cathedral. The tomb was demolished during the rebuilding of the church and Edward Marshall, the sculptor, 'tooke away the bust'. (R.S.)

404 INIGO JONES'S WILL
P.R.O.
Photograph

John Aubrey (1626–1697)
405 INIGO JONES'S TOMB IN THE
CHURCH OF ST BENET
Bodleian Library, Aubrey MSS
Photograph

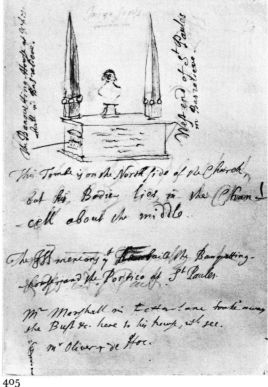

405

406   407

Portraits of Inigo Jones

Francesco Villamena (1566–1624)

406 INIGO JONES, *c.*1614
Engraving: 25·5 × 19·2
The Trustees of the Chatsworth Settlement

The earliest, least known and most revealing likeness of Inigo Jones is the engraving by Francesco Villamena, painter and engraver, possibly executed in Rome during Jones's second Italian tour. It shows Jones at about the age of 40, with tousled hair and trim moustache and beard, a prominent nose and, most telling of all, huge penetrating eyes. This engraving brilliantly captures Jones, the self-made man and revolutionary. (R.S.)

407 SELF-PORTRAIT, *c.*1615
Pen and brown ink: 10 × 6·9
The Trustees of the Chatsworth Settlement

This is the most difficult of the portraits to date, but stylistically it is definitely post-1615. The simple plain falling collar is of a type worn, with variations, since the close of Elizabeth's reign and is therefore of little help with the dating. In the same way, the nightcap also began to be worn late in the previous reign by men with balding pates. Jones's hair must have begun to thin after his return from Italy (R.S.)

408

409

408 SELF-PORTRAIT, *c.*1620
Pen and brown ink: 16 × 14
Royal Institute of British Architects

Jones is here wearing a falling ruff of *c.*1620 and a lace-edged nightcap. A useful comparison for cap and ruff is Daniel Mytens' portrait of the Duke of Richmond (1574–1624) painted shortly after the artist's arrival in England in 1618 and before the sitter's creation as Duke in 1623 (Roy Strong, *Tudor and Jacobean Portraits*, London, 1969, I, p.265; II, pl.522). (R.S.)

409 SELF-PORTRAIT, *c.*1630–1640
Pen and brown ink: 11·5 × 14·5
The Trustees of the Chatsworth Settlement

A self-portrait sketch probably made in the thirties, showing the hair and beard much more unkempt and closer in feeling to Van Dyck's drawing. (R.S.)

*Vandyke's Original Drawing, from which the Print by Van. Voerst was taken, in the
Book of Vandyke's Heads. Given me by the Duke of Devonshire.*

B Burlingte

411   412

Anthony Van Dyck (1599–1641)

410 INIGO JONES, *c.*1640

Lead: 24·2 × 19·8

The Trustees of the Chatsworth Settlement

The drawing from which Robert van Voerst made his engraving for Van Dyck's *Iconographiae*, 1640. (R.S.)

William Dobson (1610–1646)

411 INIGO JONES, *c.*1644

Oil on canvas: diameter: 59

Department of the Environment, Chiswick House

Presumably painted *c.*1644, while the court was at Oxford and certainly before Jones's capture at Basing House on October 14th, 1645. Dobson's portrait is a moving record of a sad and disillusioned old man. (R.S.)

Michael Rysbrack (1693–1770)

412 INIGO JONES, *c.*1725–30

Marble: height: 47

The Trustees of the Chatsworth Settlement

Executed for the 3rd Earl of Burlington for his villa at Chiswick, this may be after the lost tomb bust in St Benet's (405). Rysbrack made a second (now lost) for Henry Hoare at Stourhead. (R.S.)

Addenda

Le Sueur (fl. 1610–1643)

413 JAMES I

Bronze: 113 × 86·5 × 44·4

The Department of the Environment

414 CHRIST'S CHARGE TO PETER – FEED MY SHEEP, from *The Acts of the Apostles*

Mortlake tapestry: 427 × 620·2

His Grace the Duke of Buccleuch and Queensbury, K.T., G.C.V.O.

The Mortlake Tapestry Factory was founded in 1619 in imitation of Henry IV's establishment in France. Though under the official patronage of James I, the idea originated with Prince Charles and his secretary, Sir Francis Crane (359). In 1623 Prince Charles bought the Raphael Cartoons, which were the great Renaissance artist's designs for a set of tapestries to hang in the Sistine Chapel. The set woven for King Charles is now in the Mobilier National, Paris. This set with the arms of Pembroke was sold by the factory in 1638. It is not known how many sets were manufactured before the Commonwealth, but the cartoons were used again at the Restoration. The series of *The Acts of the Apostles* always remained the most highly prized product of the Mortlake Factory.

415 FIRE from *The Elements*

Mortlake tapestry: 360·9 × 719·2

His Grace the Duke of Buccleuch and Queensbury, K.T., G.C.V.O.

This is a piece from the series of the *Elements* woven for Ralph, Earl of Montagu, who was elevated to the peerage in 1688 and created a Duke in 1710. Montagu was in charge of the Mortlake Factory from 1674 until 1691, and this series was probably woven during the last years of his administration 1688–91, as his monogram with an Earl's coronet appears on the piece entitled 'Fire' from this series of the *Elements*.

416 MODEL OF WHITEHALL

Case: 155 × 160 × 40·6

The Trustees of the London Museum

Appendix I
The Provenance of Inigo Jones's Drawings

When Jones died in 1652 it was natural that his library and drawings should pass to his faithful assistant, John Webb. Webb died in 1672 and left his 'prints and Cutts and drawings of Architecture of what Nature or kindsoever' to his son William. As Webb added the proviso that nothing should be dispersed, he may have done so in the hope that his collection would remain intact beyond his son's generation. However, by about 1682 it had been partly dispersed, some to John Oliver, a master mason in the Office of Works. It is now fairly certain that what Oliver owned passed to John or William Talman, either at Oliver's death in 1701 or before, and was sold by John Talman, with all the Palladio drawings, to the 3rd Earl of Burlington in 1720 and 1721. This sale was subsequent upon William Talman's death in 1719 and must have been a transaction that was enthusiastically completed by Lord Burlington. As far as the Palladio drawings are concerned, there is no mention of them between their acquisition by Jones, presumably in 1613–15, and their sale by John Talman. It is possible therefore that they passed through other hands, but this is not likely. What remained in the Webb family probably passed to William Webb's brother, James, and thence to his wife who was a Medlicott of Ven in Somerset, not far from the Webb family seat at Butleigh. By about 1705 Dr George Clarke had acquired most of this remainder, although he did not acquire the famous annotated Palladio until 1709. He bequeathed his collections to Worcester College in 1736. In 1894 the 8th Duke of Devonshire presented to the Royal Institute of British Architects, as a gift in trust, what is now commonly called the Burlington–Devonshire Collection. This comprises the bulk of Inigo's drawings together with those by Webb that had been sold to Lord Burlington. However, the 8th Duke retained the designs for Whitehall Palace and a small number of miscellaneous designs by Webb and Jones. At some of John Talman's sales, after his death in 1728, Burlington acquired a few Jones's items, and in 1722 he had bought the masque drawings at Chatsworth from the collection of Elihu Yale. However, the masque drawings in the Royal Institute of British Architects are not part of the Burlington–Devonshire Collection, for they were given to the Institute by Anthony Salvin, sometime in the earlier part of the nineteenth century. (J.H.)

Appendix II

Notes to Gordon Toplis, *Jones's Mind and Imagination* c.f. Part II, page 61.

1 Rudolf Wittkower, *Architectural Principles in the Age of Humanism*, London, 1967, p.143

2 Ben Jonson, *Works VII: Newes from the New World*, pp.153 ff.

3 John Summerson, *Architecture in Britain 1530–1830*, Pelican 1963, p.62

4 Leone Battista Alberti, *Ten Books on Architecture*, Tr. Leoni, London, 1955, p.195

5 Plato, *The Timaeus*. The basic units are an isosceles right angled triangle and a 30° right angled triangle. These form the components of the surfaces of the Platonic solids

6 Plotinus, *The Enneads*

7 B. G. Morgan, *Light Measure and Architecture*, unpublished thesis

8 It also infiltrated from Byzantium and from Arab sources through Southern Spain

9 These included Salisbury, Buckingham, Middlesex, Arundel and Fulke Greville

10 Salomon de Caus, *Institution Harmonique Diversée en deux Parties*, Frankfurt, 1615
Henry Peacham, *The Compleat Gentleman*, London, 1622

11 D. J. Gordon, 'Poet and Architect', *Journal of the Warburg and Courtauld Institutes*, xii, 1949

12 Nikolaus Pevsner, *Academies of Art, Past and Present*, Cambridge, 1940, p.44

13 Ben Jonson, op.cit VII: Love's Welcome at Bolsover, pp.809 ff.

14 William d'Avenant, *Dramatic Works*. Ed. Maidment and Logan ii 1872, pp.327 ff.

15 Gordon Toplis, *Neo-platonic Aspects of the Thought and Work of Inigo Jones*. Unpublished thesis. These characteristics are:
   i. a comprehensive approach to architecture
   ii. laborious attention to details, especially numerical relationships; in particular, the harmonic ratios figured on the villa designs of Palladio
   iii. familiarity with many Classical authors
   iv. preoccupation with architectural precedent

16 Vitruvius, *I Dieci Libri dell'Architettura*. Comm. Barbaro, Venezia, 1567. Book i, chapter 2 and Book iv, intro.

17 Leon Battista Alberti, *L'Architettura*. Tr. Bartoli, Monreale 1565. Book ix, chapter 5

18 Vitruvius, op.cit., Book iii, chapter 1

19 Andrea Palladio, *I Quattro Libri dell'Architettura*. Venezia 1601, Book iv, chapter 25

20 John Summerson, *Inigo Jones*, Penguin 1966, p.114

21 Gordon Toplis, op.cit. In particular, the Banqueting House and the Queen's House, and in general, St Paul's Cathedral, St Paul's, Covent Garden, and number of other works. It is also worthy of note that additional harmonic ratios occur in sixteenth-century Italian musical theory. At the same time Inigo's designs of details are subject to modular organisation. Although this is not the same thing, it is further evidence of a rigorous mathematical control which is sympathetic to the ordering of the total design in terms of harmonic ratios: See also Rudolf Wittkower, *Inigo Jones, Architect and Man of Letters*, riba Journal, January 1953

22 Horace Walpole, *Anecdotes of Painting in England* . . . with additions by James Dallaway, and Vertue's catalogue of engravers who have been born or resided in England . . . revised, with additional notes by Ralph N. Wornum, London 1876

Appendix III

List of books from the library of Inigo Jones, taken from C. H. Wilkinson, 'Worcester College Library', *The Transaction of the Oxford Bibliographical Society*, 1927, pp.305, corrected and brought up to date by Dr Richard Sayce, Librarian of Worcester College.

* before a title shows that Jones wrote some notes in the book; the cases where his signature has been scored through are marked by †

1 Herodotus, *†*Herodoto Alicarnaseo Historico delle guerre de Greci & de Persi*. Translated by Mattheo Maria Boiardo. Venice, Bernardino de Bindoni, 1539, 8vo.

2 Sarayna, Torellus, *De origine et amplitudine civitatis Veronae*, Verona, Antonius Putelletus, 1540, folio

3 Fulvio, Andrea, †*Opera di Andrea Fulvio delle antichità della città di Roma*. Translated by Paulo dal Rosso. Venice, Michele Tramezino, 1543, 8vo.

4 Florus, †*Lucio Floro De fatti de Romani*. Translated by Gioan Domenico Tharsia di Capo d'Istria. Venice, heredi di Pietro de Ravani, 1546 (colophon 1547), 8vo.

5 Xenophon, *†*L'Opere morali di Xenophonte, I sette libri di Xenophonte della impresa di Ciro*. Translated by Lodovico Domenichi. Venice, Gabriel Giolito de Ferrari, 1547, 8vo.

6 Dio Cassius, *†*Dione Delle guerre de Romani*, translated by Nicolo Leoniceno. Venice, Pietro di Nicolini da Sabio, 1548, 8vo.

7 Vegetius, *† *Vegetio Dell'arte della guerra*. Translated by Francesco Ferrosi. Venice, Gabriel Giolito de Ferrari, 1551, 8vo.

8 Appian, †*Appiano Alessandrino Delle guerre civili et esterne de Romani*. Venice, figliuoli di Aldo, 1551, 8vo.

9 Aristotle, *†*L'ethica d'Aristotile*. Translated by Bernardo Segni. Venice, Bartholomeo detto l'Imperadore, 1551, 8vo.

10 Plato, *†*La Republica di Platone*. Translated by Pamphilo Fiorimbene. Venice, Gabriel Giolito de Ferrari, 1554, 8vo.

11 Curtius, Quintus, †*Q. Curtio De'fatti d'Alessandro Magno*. Translated by Thomaso Porcaschi. Venice, Gabriel Giolito de Ferrari, 1559, 4to.

12 Ptolemy, †*La geografia di Claudio Tolomeo Alessandrino*. Translated by Girolamo Ruscelli. Venice, Vincenzo Valgrisi, 1561, 4to.

13 Strabo, †*La prima parte della Geografia di Strabone*. Translated by Alfonso Buonacciuoli. Venice, Francesco Senese, 1562
**La seconda parte della Geografia di Strabone*. Ferrara, Francesco Senese, 1565

14 Alberti, Leon Battista, **L'architettura*. Translated into Italian by Cosimo Bartoli. Monte Regale, Lionardo Torrentino, 1565, folio

15 Cataneo, Pietro, *L'architettura*. Venice, Aldus, 1567, folio

16 L'Orme, Philibert de, **Le premier tome de l'Architecture*. Paris, Federic Morel, 1567, folio

17 Vasari, Giorgio, *†*Delle vite de' piu eccellenti pittori scultori et architettori*. Volume I of the Third Part. Florence, I Giunti, 1568, 4to.

18 Gamucci da san Gimignano, Bernardo, *Le antichità della città di Roma*. Venice, Giovanni Varisco, 1569, 8vo.

19 Dictys Cretensis and Dares Phrygius, **Ditte Candiotto et Darete Frigio Della guerra Troiana*, translated by Thomaso Porcacchi da Castiglione. Venice, Gabriel Giolito di Ferrarii, 1570, 4to.

20 Piccolomini, Alessandro, *†*Della institution morale*. Venice, Giordano Ziletti, 1575, 4to.

21 Euclid, †*De gli elementi d'Euclide libri quindici*. Translated by Federico Commandino. Urbino, Domenico Frisolino, 1575, folio

22 Guicciardini, Francesco, †*Dell'epitome dell'historia d'Italia*. Venice, per ordine di Iacomo Sansovino, 1580, 8vo.

23 Ubaldo, Guido, *†*Le mechaniche*. Translated by Filippo Pigafetta. Venice, Francesco di Franceschi Sanese, 1581, 4to.

24 Patricii, Francesco, †*La militia romana di Polibio, di Tito Livio, e di Dionizi Alicarnaseo*. Ferrara, Domenico Mamarelli, 1583, 4to.

25 [Palladio, Andrea], *Le cose maravigliose dell'alma città di Roma* includes *L'antichità di Roma di M. Andrea Paladio*. Venice, Girolamo Francino, 1588, 8vo.

26 Vasari, Giorgio, †*Ragionamenti*. Florence, Filippo Giunti, 1588. 4to.

27 Alberti, Leandro, †*Descrittione di tutta Italia*. Venice, Altobello Salicato, 1588, 4to.

28 Bordinus, Iohannes Franciscus, *De rebus praeclare gestis a Sixto V Pon. Max*. Rome, Iacobus Tornerius, 1588, 4to.

29 Rusconi, Giovanni Antonio, *Della Architettura*. Venice, I Gioliti, 1590, folio

30 Cartari, Vincenzo, †*Le imagini de i dei de gli antichi*. Venice, Marc' Antonio Zaltieri, 1592, 4to.

31 Palladio, Andrea, *I quattro libri dell'architettura*. Venice, Bartolomeo Carampello, 1601, folio

32 Summonte, Giovanni Antonio, †*Historia della citta e regno di Napoli*. Two volumes. Naples, Giovanni Iacomo Carlino, 1602–1601, 4to.

33 Scala, Giovanni, †*Geometria prattica . . . sopra le tauole dell'Ecc^te Mathematico Giovanni Pomodoro*. Rome, Giovanni Martinelli, 1603, folio

33a Plutarch, †*Vite di Plutarco Cheroneo de gli Roumini illutstri(sic) Greci et Romani*. Translated by Lodovico Domenichi. Venice, Bartolomeo de gli Alberti, 1607, 4to.

34 Lorini, Buonaiuto, *Le fortificationi*. Venice, Francesco Rampazetto, 1609, folio

35 Plutarch, *†*Opuscoli morali, di Plutarco Cheronese*. Translated by Marc' Antonio Gandino. Venice, Fioravante Prati, 1614, 4to.

36 Scamozzi, Vincenzo, *†*L'idea della architettura universale*. Two volumes. Venice, at the expense of the author, 1615, folio

37 Caesar, Julius, *I commentari di C. Giulio Cesare, con le figure in rame . . . Fatte da Andrea Palladio*. Venice, Girolamo Foglietti, 1598, 4to.

38 Busca, Gabriello, *†*L'architettura militare*. Milan, Giovanni Battista Bidelli, 1619, 4to.

39 Viola Zanini, Gioseffe, *Delle architettura*. Padua, Francesco Bolzetta, 1629, 4to.

43 Xenophon, †*Xenophonte Della vita di Cyro re de Persi*. Translated by Iacopo di Messer Poggio Fiorentino. Florence, gli heredi di Philippe di Giunta, 1521, 8vo.

44 Vignola, Giacomo Barozzi da, *Regola delli cinque ordini d'architettura*. Rome, Andreas Vaccarius, 1607, folio

45 Plutarch, *†*Alcuni opusculi de le cose morali del divino Plutarco*. Venice, Comin da Trino di Monferrato, 1567, 8vo.

46 Polybius, *Les cinq premiers livres des Histoires de Polybe Megalopolitein*. Translated by Louis Maigret. Lyons, Jean de Tournes, 1558, folio

Bibliographical Sources

General

J. Alfred Gotch, *Inigo Jones*, 1928

John Harris, *Catalogue of the Drawings Collection of the Royal Institute of British Architects: Inigo Jones and John Webb*, 1972

John Harris and A. Tait, *Catalogue of Drawings by Inigo Jones, John Webb and Isaac de Caus in the Collection of Worcester College, Oxford* (forthcoming)

James Lees-Milne, *The Age of Inigo Jones*, 1953

John Nichols, *Progresses of James I*, 1828

Stephen Orgel and Roy Strong, *Inigo Jones, The Theatre of the Stuart Court*, 1973

Richard Southern, *Changeable Scenery*, 1952

John Summerson, *Inigo Jones*, 1966

John Summerson, *History of the King's Works* (ed. H. M. Colvin), III (forthcoming)

Part I: Jones in the Making

The Early Years: 1573–1605

INIGO JONES'S FAMILY

Parish Registers of St Bartholomew the Less, St Bartholomew's Hospital

J. Alfred Gotch, *Inigo Jones*, 1928

JONES'S EARLY TRAVELS: 1598(?)–1604(?)

John Webb, *A Vindication of Stone-Heng, Restored*, 1665, pp.122–24

Complete Peerage, ed. Vycary Gibbs, s.v. Ros or Roos

The Festival Tradition

Roy Strong, 'Inigo Jones and the Revival of Chivalry', *Apollo*, LXXXVI, 1967, pp.102–107

Per Palme, 'Ut Architectura Poesis', *Acta Universitatis Upsaliensis*, in *Figura*, new series, I, pp.95–107

The Architectural Tradition

Mark Girouard, *Robert Smythson and the Architecture of the Elizabethan Era*, 1966

Eric Mercer, *English Art, 1553–1625*, Oxford 1962

The Jacobean Romantic: Jones and Robert Cecil, Earl of Salisbury

L. Stone, 'The Building of Hatfield House', *Archaeological Journal*, CXII, 1956, pp.100–128

L. Stone, 'Inigo Jones and the New Exchange', *Archaeological Journal*, CXIV, 1957, pp.106–121

John Newman, 'An early drawing by Inigo Jones and a monument in Shropshire', *Burlington Magazine*, no.843, 1973

Scott McMillin, 'Jonson's Early Entertainments, New Information from Hatfield House', *Renaissance Drama*, new series, I, 1968, pp.153–166

Stephen Orgel and Roy Strong, *Inigo Jones, The Theatre of the Stuart Court*, 1973

Jones and Anne of Denmark: 1605–1611

THE EARLY MASQUES AND ENTERTAINMENTS

Stephen Orgel and Roy Strong, *Inigo Jones, The Theatre of the Stuart Court*, 1973

THE VISIT TO FRANCE, 1609

Calendar of State Papers, Domestic

In the Service of Henry, Prince of Wales: 1610–1612

SURVEYOR TO THE PRINCE

John Summerson, *History of the King's Works* (ed. H. M. Colvin), III (forthcoming)

Accounts:
Richmond: P.R.O. SP 14/64 no.64
St James's Palace: P.R.O. E 351/3244

THE PRINCE'S FESTIVALS

Stephen Orgel and Roy Strong, *Inigo Jones, The Theatre of the Stuart Court*, 1973

The Wedding of the Princess Elizabeth and the Elector Palatine: 1613

Stephen Orgel and Roy Strong, *Inigo Jones, The Theatre of the Stuart Court*, 1973

The Second Italian Journey: 1613–1615

M. Hervey, *Life of Thomas Howard, Earl of Arundel*, 1921

W. G. Keith, 'Inigo Jones as a Collector', RIBA *Journal*, XXXIII, December 1925–6, pp.95–108

J. Alfred Gotch, 'Inigo Jones's principal visit to Italy in 1614: The Itinerary of his journeys', RIBA *Journal*, XLIV, 1937, 1007–1008

A. Tait, 'Inigo Jones – Architectural Historian', *Burlington Magazine*, CXII, 1970, pp.235

Part II The British Vitruvius

Jones as a Draughtsman

J. Sumner Smith, 'The Italian Sources of Inigo Jones's Style', *Burlington Magazine*, XCIV, 1952, pp.200–207

Stephen Orgel and Roy Strong, *Inigo Jones, The Theatre of the Stuart Court*, 1973

Jones's Mind and Imagination

C. Rowe, *The Theoretical Drawings of Inigo Jones, their Sources and Scope.* Unpublished University of London thesis, 1947

Gordon Toplis, *Neo-platonic Aspects of the Thought and Work of Inigo Jones.* Unpublished thesis

R. Wittkower, *Architectural Principles in the Age of Humanism*, 1967

B. G. Morgan, *Light, Measure and Architecture.* Unpublished thesis

Anthony Blunt, *Artistic Theory in Italy 1450–1600*, 1956

Jones's Library

C. H. Wilkinson, 'Worcester College Library', *The Transactions of the Oxford Bibliographical Society*, 1927, pp.305

Jones as a Connoisseur

R. Wittkower, 'Inigo Jones: Puritissimo fiero', *Burlington Magazine*, XC, 1948

'Abraham van der Dort's Catalogue of the Collections of Charles I', ed. O. Millar, *Walpole Society*, XXXVII, 1960

'The Inventories and Valuations of the King's Goods 1649–51', ed. O. Millar, *Walpole Society*, XLII, 1972

Sources for Jones's Masque Designs

Stephen Orgel and Roy Strong, *Inigo Jones, The Theatre of the Stuart Court*, 1973

Jones and Stonehenge

Stephen Orgel, 'Inigo Jones on Stonehenge', *Prose*, III (forthcoming)

The Mechanical Development of Jones's Stage

F. A. Yates, *Theatre of the World*, 1969

Stephen Orgel and Roy Strong, *Inigo Jones, The Theatre of the Stuart Court*, 1973

Richard Southern, *Changeable Scenery*, 1952

Part III: The King's Arcadia

Jones and Anne of Denmark: The Last Years, 1615–1619

G. H. Chettle, *The Queen's House, Greenwich*, 1937

M. Whinney, 'An Unknown Design for a Villa by Inigo Jones', *The Country Seat*, ed. H. M. Colvin and John Harris, 1970, pp.33–5

John Summerson, *History of the King's Works* (ed. H. M. Colvin), III (forthcoming)

W. G. Keith, 'The Palace of Oatlands', *Archaeological Review*, XXXIX, 1916, pp.76–7

John Nichols, *Progresses of James I*, 1828

ACCOUNTS:

Funeral: P.R.O. L.C.2/5; A.C.1/391/59

Arundel, Jones and the Italian Style

M. Hervey, *Life of Thomas Howard, Earl of Arundel*, 1921

John Harris, *Catalogue of the Drawings Collection of the Royal Institute of British Architects: Inigo Jones and John Webb*, 1972

John Harris and A. Tait, *Catalogue of Drawings by Inigo Jones, John Webb and Isaac de Caus in the Collection of Worcester College, Oxford* (forthcoming)

John Harris, 'Inigo and the Courtier Style', *Architectural Review*, CLIV, July 1973, pp.17–24

Surveyor to the Crown: Part I, 1615–1625

John Harris, *Catalogue of the Drawings Collection of the Royal Institute of British Architects: Inigo Jones and John Webb*, 1972

John Harris and A. Tait, *Catalogue of Drawings by Inigo Jones, John Webb and Isaac de Caus in the Collection of Worcester College, Oxford* (forthcoming)

John Summerson, *History of the King's Works* (ed. H. M. Colvin), III (forthcoming)

John Harris, 'Inigo Jones and the Prince's Lodging at Newmarket', *Architectural History*, 2, 1959, pp.26–40

Per Palme, *Triumph of Peace: A study of the Whitehall Banqueting House*, Stockholm, 1956

J. J. Terwen, 'De plattegronden voor het Banqueting House in Whitehall', *Opstellen voor H. van de Waal*, Amsterdam, 1970

O. Millar, *Rubens: The Whitehall Ceiling*, Oxford, 1958

ACCOUNTS:
Newmarket: P.R.O. E351/3251–3252–3253
Banqueting House: P.R.O. E 351/3391 and for many others cf. John Summerson, *History of the King's Works*
Marquess of Buckingham's First Lodging: P.R.O. E 351/3252
Marquess of Buckingham's Second Lodging: P.R.O. E 351/3253
St James's Chapel: P.R.O. E 351/3260

House of Lords: P.R.O. E 351/3257–3258
Greenwich Chapel: P.R.O. E 351/3257

Masques for Charles, Prince of Wales, 1616–1635

Stephen Orgel and Roy Strong, *Inigo Jones, The Theatre of the Stuart Court*, 1973

The Funeral of James I, 1625

John Summerson, *History of the King's Works* (ed. H. M. Colvin), III (forthcoming)

John Harris and A. Tait, *Catalogue of Drawings by Inigo Jones, John Webb and Isaac de Caus in the Collection of Worcester College, Oxford* (forthcoming)

John Nichols, *Progresses of James I*, 1828

ACCOUNTS: P.R.O. L.C.2/6

Surveyor to the Crown: Part II, 1625–1640

For general references, see works cited in Part I

John Summerson, *Inigo Jones*, British Academy Lecture, 1964 (for Covent Garden and St Paul's Cathedral)

Margaret Whinney, 'John Webb's Drawings for Whitehall Palace', *Walpole Society*, XXXI, 1946, pp.45–108

John Harris, 'Inigo Jones and his French Sources', *The Metropolitan Museum of Art Bulletin*, May, 1961, pp.253–264

G. E. Bentley, *The Jacobean and Caroline Stage*, VI, 1968, pp.267–288 (for the Whitehall Cockpit)

ACCOUNTS:
St James's Palace Gateway: P.R.O. E 351/3265
Whitehall Cockpit: P.R.O.351/3263–3264–3267
St Paul's Cathedral: Cathedral Library W.A.1–15; Lambeth Palace Library for W.A.12

Jones and Henrietta Maria

THE ARCHITECTURE

John Harris, *Catalogue of the Drawings Collection of the Royal Institute of British Architects: Inigo Jones and John Webb*, 1972

John Summerson, *History of the King's Works* (ed. H. M. Colvin) III (forthcoming)

C. S. S. Higham, *Wimbledon Manor under the Cecils*, 1962

R. Needham and A. Webster, *Somerset House Past and Present*, 1909

ACCOUNTS:
Somerset House: P.R.O. E 351/3262–3263–3264–3265–3269; P.R.O. A.O.I./2490, 383;
P.R.O. Works 30/260

cf. Sir Richard Wynn's accounts in the National Library of Wales, Wynn Papers nos. 161–186 (for Wimbledon and Oatlands also)

THE PLAYS

Stephen Orgel and Roy Strong, *Inigo Jones, The Theatre of the Stuart Court*, 1973

The Royal Masques: 1631–1640

Stephen Orgel and Roy Strong, *Inigo Jones, The Theatre of the Stuart Court*, 1973

Jones and Civic Architecture

John Summerson, *Inigo Jones*, British Academy Lecture, 1964 (for Covent Garden and St Paul's Cathedral)

Survey of London, 1970, *St Paul's Covent Garden*, pp.19–128

Jones and Country Houses

James Lees-Milne, *The Age of Inigo Jones*, 1953

Oliver Hill and John Cornforth, *English Country Houses: Caroline 1625–1685*, 1966

PARTICULAR BUILDINGS:

H. M. Colvin, 'The South Front of Wilton House', *Archaeological Journal*, CXI, 1954, pp.181–190
A. Tait, 'Isaac de Caus and the South Front of Wilton', *Burlington Magazine*, CVI, 1964, p.74
John Harris, 'Raynham Hall, Norfolk', *Archaeological Journal*, CXVII, 1963, pp.180–187

Jones's Architectural and Theatrical Legacy

ARCHITECTURAL

James Lees-Milne, *The Age of Inigo Jones*, 1953

THEATRICAL

Richard Southern, *Changeable Scenery*, 1952

The Surveyor's Last Years: 1640–1652

J. Alfred Gotch, *Inigo Jones*, 1928

John Harris, 'Inigo and the Courtier Style', *Architectural Review*, CLIV, July 1973, pp.17–24

Index of Lenders

Photographic Index

(unless otherwise stated, the sources are in London)

Diagrams 45, 146, 148, 150, 153, 155, 156, 162 by permission of Westerham Press, artwork by Paul Sharp

General Index

of artists, sitters, patrons, places, authors and their works. Architectural works by Inigo Jones are found by place name and designs for masques under author and title of the masque. The index is not exhaustive. References are to page numbers.